NOBBUT A LAD

Also by Alan Titchmarsh

FICTION

Mr MacGregor

The Last Lighthouse Keeper

Animal Instincts

Only Dad

Rosie

Love and Dr Devon

NON-FICTION INCLUDES

Alan Titchmarsh's Favourite Gardens

Gardener's World Complete Book of Gardening

How to be a Gardener Book One: Back to Basics

How to be a Gardener Book Two: Secrets of Success

The Gardener's Year

British Isles: A Natural History

Trowel and Error

NOBBUT A LAD

A Yorkshire Childhood

Written and Illustrated by Alan Titchmarsh

HODDER &
STOUGHTON

Copyright © 2006 by Alan Titchmarsh

First published in Great Britain in 2006 by Hodder & Stoughton
A division of Hodder Headline

The right of Alan Titchmarsh to be identified as the Author
of the Work has been asserted by him in accordance with
the Copyright, Designs and Patents Act 1988.

A Hodder & Stoughton Book

1

A CIP catalogue record for this title is available from the British Library

Hardback ISBN 978 0 340 83117 5
ISBN 0 340 83117 0
Trade paperback ISBN 978 0 340 93337 4
ISBN 0 340 93337 2

Typeset in Bembo by Hewer Text UK Ltd, Edinburgh
Printed and bound by Clays Ltd, St Ives plc

Hodder Headline's policy is to use papers that are natural, renewable
and recyclable products and made from wood grown in sustainable
forests. The logging and manufacturing processes are expected to
conform to the environmental regulations of the country of origin.

Hodder & Stoughton Ltd
A division of Hodder Headline
338 Euston Road
London NW1 3BH

Endpapers: Detail from *Bartholomew Survey Atlas of England and Wales*, 1939.

For Polly and Camilla, with love as always

Contents

Contents

Foreword

A friend asked me if I was using people's real names. There was a note of warning in his voice. 'What if they get upset?'

It did concern me. I contemplated replacing each one with a pseudonym just to be on the safe side, but where would it all end? The temptation would then be to change facts to suit. And to embroider a bit. Could I actually make it more of a novel? It was an attractive proposition. I could spice it up a bit then. But having written one volume of memoirs – *Trowel and Error* – in which people appeared under their real names, it seemed somehow dishonest to suddenly go all coy and call them something else.

I don't think there is anything libellous here, though a few school friends might not always see things quite the way I did. I hope they'll forgive me. My memories of them may well have been coloured by the passing of time in pretty much the same way as their memories of me. Only where the use of a real name would have caused genuine embarrassment and discomfort have I changed it, and even then, very rarely.

My English teacher, Miss Weatherall, who turned eighty this year and about whom I was not especially kind in *Trowel and Error*, wrote to thank me for the birthday card I sent her, and at the same time admonished me for what she perceived as inaccuracies in my reporting of events. She said that the only reason she didn't sue me was that I could afford to lose and she couldn't. While not entirely agreeing with her sentiments, I appreciate her generosity of spirit and hope that other people I encountered in my childhood will be similarly forbearing. As Dame Edith Sitwell remarked, 'There is no truth, only points of view.'

This book is not strictly chronological, and neither is it a detailed memoir like *Trowel and Error*. It is more a series of tales from childhood. The occurrences described all took place, though in the interests of a smooth narrative I have occasionally compressed a series of events or arranged them in a different order. It is a relatively gentle read of a relatively gentle Yorkshire childhood in the 1950s. It is not overly peppered with 'Si thee's and 'Wee'r's ta goin'?'s by way of giving it local colour. My parents were both Yorkshire born and bred, but they resented any implication that it somehow meant that they had to speak only in the local dialect. My dad did indeed say 'Y'alreet?' when enquiring after a friend's health and 'Na then' when passing someone in the street, but he would not have said either on meeting the Queen or to a lady 'up the Grove' whose lavatory he was repairing. Both my sister and I have Yorkshire accents (my vowels now rather more rounded than hers after thirty-odd years 'down South'), but we were not allowed to use bad grammar. Much as it might make for a more interesting read, I can't claim that we suffered extreme poverty or, at the other end of the scale, great privileges. I was not born into a persecuted minority, nor was I neglected or abused – apart from the odd clip round the ear.

Mum and Dad were ordinary working class when it came to their position on the social scale, but extraordinary when it came to their effect on my sister and me. I don't think any children could have been, in turn, more devoted to, influenced by, exasperated by, loved and better served by a plumber and his wife who quietly got on with their lives and gave their children a chance to get on with theirs in whatever way they chose – provided they knew where we were, what we were doing and who we were doing it with.

There were rules; there were standards, but there was no hint of snobbery or social climbing – apart from my mother's inherent dislike of ITV (common) and the belief that certain things were 'not nice' – and my sister and I were brought up to believe in such hackneyed principles as 'Do as you would be done by' and 'If you can't say anything nice about somebody, then don't say anything at all'. This last maxim wasn't always adhered to by my mum, but then another of her favourites was 'It's do as I say, not as I do'.

She was a woman of unaccountable prejudices. She adored the doctor, tripe and vinegar, and a drop of Bell's Scotch whisky. She disliked Geordies, flirty women (being one herself), chewing gum and cream soda. But in spite of her little foibles, she was a good mother and, by today's standards, relatively strict.

She didn't, I hope, turn us into little goody-goodies. But along with my dad – the quieter of the two in that classic way of many Yorkshire couples – she did, somehow, give us a fairly optimistic outlook on life, and imbued us with a sense of responsibility for those around us. Not in a relentlessly holier-than-thou way, but in that 'Get on with it and stop making a fuss' way that prevailed in the 1950s.

We were never encouraged to think that we were better than anybody else. If anything, we were taught that we were just the same. The most important thing in life seemed to be to blend in and get on with everybody, and I suppose that's what I've spent the rest of my life doing. Blending in.

I don't think these are sentiments that were confined to our household, though I do, from time to time, encounter people who look at me as though I'm from another planet.

Judge for yourself.

In terms of bodily constitution I don't suppose it makes a ha'p'orth of difference where you are born, but I'm glad that I took my first breath of air on the moors. It was in a stone-built maternity home called St Winifred's. I'd like to think she was the patron saint of children – or gardeners – but she wasn't. They get St Nicholas and St Fiacre respectively. The Oxford Dictionary of Saints *only offers St Winefride, a Welsh virgin, and there weren't many of those in Ilkley. The building stands by the paddling pool on the very edge of the moor at the top of Wells Road. It's a block of flats now, but before it was even a maternity home, it was a private house, and Charles Darwin was staying there when he heard from his publisher that* The Origin of Species *was a commercial success. Or so I heard. It's the kind of fact that I'd like to believe.*

I was born at nine o'clock in the evening on 2 May 1949 to Alan (plumber of this parish) and Bessie Titchmarsh (née Hardisty) in a heatwave, and my mum had a bit of a struggle. 'I almost burst a blood vessel,' she would say confidentially when pressed for details. They clearly decided that one child was enough, until time had healed the wound. That would account for the fact that my sister, Kath, arrived almost five years later, so for the toddling years I was on my own.

Early On

'Now look what you've done. You've made him cry.'

I wish that the first words I remember hearing had been more positive. Less suggestive of an oversensitive nature. They were spoken by my maternal grandmother, Kitty Hardisty, and directed at my mum. We were in Grandma's sitting room at 46 Ash Grove. The one that was never used. The one with the glass domes of stuffed birds and the crystal lustre candlesticks on the mantelpiece. I can't have been very old. One and a half, maybe two. And it can't have been that difficult to have made me cry.

My mum wasn't naturally cruel. Strict, yes, but not cruel, and I can only guess that it was the sound of raised voices that moved me to tears. Some trivial family disagreement. Whether to have chops or fish for tea. Nothing more. But then I've never been good with raised voices, especially from those close to me.

And that's about the extent of my mistreatment as a child. A few raised voices. Those and a couple of swipes on the bum with a whalebone hairbrush, after which Dad would have to go out into the garden for a cigarette, racked with guilt.

It took him days to get over it, my mother told me later. It probably took me rather less.

I read of other writers' early lives with just a tinge of envy – all those drunken fathers and irresponsible mothers; of children deserted or repressed. I don't for one fleeting moment wish I'd shared their lot, neither am I unsympathetic to their plight, but it does impart a certain cathartic quality to their writing that I suppose mine lacks.

I am not naturally pessimistic. Whenever I'm asked, by some newspaper interviewer, what is the worst thing that's ever happened to me, my mind goes blank. I can never think of anything that might be acceptable, except for the loss of my parents, and that seems far too heavy for their needs. Most of the 'little local difficulties' along the way I've expunged from my memory. It seems more rewarding to save space for happier recollections.

I'm also deeply influenced by the traditional northern ethic that 'There's always somebody worse off than yourself'; I've been happy to espouse this in the sure and certain belief that if I do think I'm having a rough time and complain about it, then the hand of fate will be happy to prove to me that if I think this is bad, just wait until I see what's round the corner.

Maybe I'm too secretive to admit to being unhappy. Or too thick-skinned to have been deeply affected by misfortune. The latter I know to be untrue, the former I'm nervous of admitting, but I know that I do have a tendency to make the best of a bad job, to avoid complaining (except to my most intimate friends) and to put a brave face on it.

Does this make me dishonest? Or shallow? Is it better to dissect bitter feelings and lay them bare for the benefit of others than to soldier on and forget they ever happened? Not in my case.

But there I can blame my mother again. At the end of her life, her mobility curbed by arthritis, her once-beautiful hands swollen and deformed and most of her body gripped by pain, she would answer the question 'How are you?' with a single word: 'Fine.'

And I suppose most of us are 'fine'. A bit battered by this and that. A bit bruised. A bit odd. But basically fine. And growing up in a pleasant town in the Yorkshire Dales in the 1950s was, for a child who liked to be out of doors, the best of all possible worlds.

Not that it was without incident, or occasional tragedy. But that's growing up. And growing up, even in the best of all possible worlds, is a confusing thing to have to do.

I was given my father's name at my christening – Alan – as well as my paternal grandfather's – Fred – but to avoid confusion at home, where there were now two Alans, I was known as 'Sparrow' by my mum and 'Algy' by my dad. Later on, when I was of an age to read The Eagle, *Dad would call me 'Digby' or 'Dig' – after Dan Dare's sidekick. My sister calls me 'Ala'. Always has.*

Things could have been very different. My mother favoured the name Rodney until put off by the doctor: 'For God's sake, don't call him that.' She adjusted it to Robin, but when I was born she was clearly overtaken by a wave of sentiment and called me after my dad.

My mum had no sympathy when I complained that the name Alan led to me being confused with my father, and that Fred was a rotten middle name that everyone poked fun at. She hated her own name, Bessie, saying that it was only ever given to cows and fire engines. Her family called her 'Bet'. Dad called her 'Beff'. Always.

The Outsider

I seemed always to be out of doors, and if not actually under the sky, then certainly within spitting distance of it. Mum always had the back door open, come rain or shine. Nowadays it would be called claustrophobia, but throughout her life she would have none of that and put it down to the fact that 'I can't do with being fast', meaning that she couldn't bear to feel that she was enclosed. Which is called claustrophobia.

There wasn't a lot of sky where we lived, not compared with East Anglia. Apart from the terraced houses, which got in the way, if you looked to the south, you would see the moors rising upwards – green in spring, purple in summer and brown in winter – and to the north Middleton Woods. The River Wharfe ran between them in the bottom of the valley.

In all but the worst of weathers, my massive pram would be parked outside the back door; the door that in summer was hung with a deckchair-striped curtain on specially fitted hooks to prevent the sun from causing the woodgrain-effect paint to blister. Dulux was in its infancy. The three back steps were built of stone, freshly edged with a line of creamy-white chalk once a week. It was done for show, but there was a practical side to it as well. There was no street lighting down the back, and with white edges to the steps there was less chance of you tripping up over them and measuring your length; especially if you came home late having had a couple, though the chances are that then you would have used the front door, where the steps were chalked in the same way. For a few years, anyway. Then it wore off – the habit, not the chalk. Some folk painted their steps all over in red lead. Dad quite liked the idea, and even brought a large tin of the stuff home from work. But Mum thought that for outside that was a bit too ostentatious (one of her favourite words) and got him to paint the kitchen floor with it instead. For the next two years we shimmied around on the glossy red flagstones like dancers at the Tower Ballroom in Blackpool.

You could come in and out of the front door if you were wearing smart clothes, otherwise you used the one round the back that led into the kitchen. If my dad came home for his lunch in his overalls, he could eat it at the Fablon-covered breakfast bar that he'd made in the kitchen, and then he was allowed to flop in his armchair in the front room for his cup of tea, but only if a newspaper was laid over the chair first. And he had to take his cap off and drink out of the cup, not the saucer, however hot the tea might be. My mum did have standards, and although her dad drank his tea out of the saucer, it was not something that was encouraged in her own house.

In those early days Mum was a creature of habit. Monday was washday, Tuesday was ironing, Wednesday and Thursday were cleaning, Friday was baking, Saturday was shopping and Sunday we went out for a walk.

The code by which we lived was, by today's standards, rigorous and enforced. It wasn't of the joyless ascetic variety, but there were just ways of doing things. Proper ways. Respectable ways. If someone in the street died, everyone would draw their curtains. Those who didn't were regarded as being, at best, thoughtless and, at worst, downright rude.

Mum's favourite word for inconsiderateness in other women was 'sackless', and women of whom she disapproved were known as 'that dame'.

On Nelson Road, our very ordinary little street of stone terraced houses, the niceties of life were observed almost as fastidiously as they must have been in Jane Austen's England. When a funeral cortège went by, you didn't carry on walking, but stood still until it had passed. Gentlemen raised their hats, and boys their school caps. If I forgot, I would feel a dig in the ribs. 'Algy – cap!'

At all times men walked on the outside of the pavement, ladies on the inside. I still do, even though it does sometimes cause confusion when after crossing the road, the woman I am walking with discovers that I'm not where I was. It's not that we ever made a big thing of it; it was taken for granted. It still is.

When we went out for walks on a Sunday, Dad wore a collar and tie, his new grey gaberdine coat and his best cap; my mum, my sister and I wore coats that Mum had made – only Dad's was bought from Greenwood's.

Under the shade of the flowering currant bush by the back door, and next door to Dad's bike, which was leaned against the back wall of the house and shrouded in a bit of old stair carpet, I'd be parked in my pram to take the air; fastened in with a pair of reins to stop me from climbing over the side. While Mum busied herself in the back kitchen, I could squint in the bright sunlight at the blackbird nesting in the sycamore tree that grew only slightly higher than the stone-built midden, and stare wide-eyed at Dennis Petty, the black-faced coalman, as he lifted up the iron grating and rattled the contents of his half-hundredweight sacks down the chute that led to the cellar. A plume of black dust would spiral into the air as each sack went from being plump to empty, and the sneezes that followed would cloud my eyes with tears.

Every day I could watch Podgy, the black-and-white cat from two doors up, as he stalked the blackbird (he could never move fast enough to catch it, but then he wasn't called Podgy for nothing), and once a week be terrified by the noise and smell of the pigswill man.

Old Mr Petty, Dennis's dad, would come in his wellies and overalls to empty the short, fat, metal bins that sat next to the dustbins down the back, where people put their potato peelings, stale bread and leftover food. Not that there was a lot of that. Plates were cleared at most meals. He'd tip the contents of the bins into a larger one with a handle that he would then heave up on to his back, and walk past my pram leaving the sickly-sweet stench of pigswill hovering in the air, to mix with the acrid tang of the bruised currant leaves that his shoulder had caught rounding the corner. I never saw his pigs; I think he kept them down by the allotments.

In that no-man's-land between the backyard and the garden – 'the back' – there would be comings and goings all day long. Wives and widows going out to the shops in their thick coats, with dark felt hats held on with huge pins. Kids would learn to ride their bikes here, bumping over the uneven ground that sloped from the top of the back to the bottom and sometimes landing in the hedges that fronted the small back gardens where cabbages grew, and Brussels sprouts. There were savoys and sometimes a few onions, but never leeks or marrows or anything remotely exotic – only 'greens'. You knew where you were with them and they kept you regular.

There were no lawns, just patches of rough grass where a pram could be parked, or a painted kitchen chair perched on the hottest days of summer when top buttons of blouses would be undone and a glass of orange squash would take the place of tea. Neither were there elaborate flower borders, just the odd rose bush or hydrangea or maybe a couple of overgrown blackcurrant bushes. A bit of honeysuckle might run up into a scrawny tree and scent the air with its heavy perfume when spring turned into summer.

The Cawoods had a large Bramley apple tree; the Dinsdales had enough old floorboards and planks to start a timber yard; and Mr Barker had a shed for his motorbike and sidecar, and a miniature version for his tortoises, Tommy and Thomas.

Other gardens were dark and mysterious – their privet hedges having long since grown outwards and skywards to swallow up the narrow strip of land, and at the end of the nine houses, at the very bottom of the back loomed the orange brick wall of Ledgard's bus garage.

The blue-and-black buses and coaches would come and go at the beginning and end of the day – off to Leeds and Bradford, Otley and

Skipton. Samuel Ledgard's double-deckers were not as luxurious as the bright-red ones of the West Yorkshire Road Car Company, who operated from the centre of town, but their coaches, said my mum, were 'much comfier'.

Next to the bus garage, in the end house, lived Mrs Beaumont, who looked a hundred and fifty. She wasn't much taller than us kids, her teeth were long gone, and she wore a black dress that reached down to the ground, with a large white apron and a mob cap like some serving woman from an Elizabethan banquet. She never said much, and when she did, it was usually to tell an unwanted caller to go away. I tried to be nice to her once, in that eager-to-please, childish sort of way. Nothing too earnest, just a smile and a hello. She told me to piss off, so I did, trying not to feel crushed. Some weeks afterwards she retreated into the house and quietly died.

Mrs Lettern was next up; a widow with horn-rimmed glasses and a spiky felt hat; a bit dour and almost as antisocial as Mrs Beaumont. Then came the Cawoods, an old couple with several grown-up children and the youngest, Pauline, who at my age was obviously a late arrival. It seemed odd that Pauline's mum and dad were so old, when mine were so young – just 25 when I was born. Mr Cawood was particularly shaky on his pins, and in September you could see his wife in her floral pinny, with her grey forties-style hair, steadying his bottom as he stood on a chair below the apple tree and hooked down the fruit with the handle of his walking stick. I was convinced that one day he'd fall and break his neck. That's what you did when you fell out of an apple tree. In the end he died of natural causes. It was all a bit disappointing.

The Evanses had a boy and a girl – Winton (grammar school and a bit aloof) and Jane (keen on ballet but no threat to Fonteyn). The Barkers next door to them were childless – she a martyr to nervous headaches, and he a special constable who directed traffic on bank-holiday weekends. (I burned my leg on his motorbike radiator and had to have soap rubbed on it to take away the sting. It didn't work.)

Then came the Pettys – Dennis, the coalman with the black face, and Joan his wife, with ash-blonde hair and skirts that my mother said were far too short. My dad said nothing. I could see him smiling behind the *Daily Express*. Mrs Petty looked like Gaye Gambol. Their daughter, Virginia, with hair not quite as blonde as her mum's and longer skirts, was my first girlfriend. The first one who bought me a Christmas present, anyway – a box of New Berry Fruits. I think she ran up to Thornber's – the top shop (as opposed to Morgan's, the bottom shop) – to get them after I'd sent her a box of Maltesers. But it didn't matter that it was an afterthought. At least she cared enough to bother.

Mrs Cunnington was next door to us. She was a dumpling of a woman and a widow by the time I was six or seven. She was also our favourite neighbour – kindly and warm, with a nice line in hums. She knew when my mother had stood me in the corner for being naughty because she could hear me kicking the skirting board.

'Have-it's in trouble again,' she'd mutter to herself. She called me 'Have-it' when I was little on account of my fascination with her trinkets. Mrs Cunnington had a lot of knick-knacks, towards which I would totter with arms outstretched saying, 'Have it. Have it.'

'Cookie' she was always called, apparently because I couldn't say 'Cunnington' when I was little. As a result, the entire street called her 'Cookie'. She was, said my mother, a cockney from Croydon (to my mother, anyone who lived south of Derby was a cockney), and though she had lived in Yorkshire for most of her life, her accent was still that of a Londoner. 'All right, duck?' she'd ask. And when someone was cross, she'd say, 'He played Hamlet,' or, 'He played billy-o'; expressions that were clearly not of Yorkshire origin.

She had a brother called Rex who came to see her occasionally. He wore bow ties, had rimless glasses and a grey moustache and spoke posh, and his wife – 'Verie', never Vera – hardly ever spoke to us. I think we were a bit beneath her. She lived in Harrogate.

Cookie was an amazing shape. She was not so much round as amorphous. Her breasts were large but undefined and, under the grey cardigan she always wore, they disappeared into her hips. It seems unkind to describe her like this, but as a child her anatomy gave me cause for much curiosity. Her legs came out of the bottom of a full skirt held at some distance from them by her pannier-like hips, and were usually terminated by a pair of brown slippers with a pompom on each foot. I caught a glimpse of her knees once. They erupted above the short stockings that were held in place with elastic, and looked like a collection of white apples in a small sack. Her hair was grey and fastened into a hairnet at the back with kirby grips, and she had glasses and a rather squashed face. But she was kind – a bit like a favourite granny – and babysat for me and my sister when Mum and Dad fancied a night out. When she kissed you goodnight, her skin was soft and warm, not cold and prickly like some of Dad's aunties. He had seven of them, and Auntie Ethel was the prickliest in temperament as well as kiss.

Cookie's husband – 'Cookin' – died when I was little, so for the majority of my childhood she lived alone, sitting in a huge wooden Windsor chair alongside the big black range in her front room, where she'd bake bread and heat up the kettle in between making rag rugs and taking cuttings of busy Lizzies.

We had a range, too, when we first arrived at Nelson Road, but it was soon replaced with a small fireplace made of mottled cream tiles. Cookie's room always seemed warmer somehow, and friendlier, but we were much more up to date.

She didn't do much with her garden ('It's my hips, duck'), but she was a dab hand with the plants on her windowsill. There were spider plants and succulents – money plants and partridge-breasted aloes that she called 'my pheasant's breast' – and a forest of busy Lizzies. Cookie was the first person I knew who had green fingers. She was forever rooting cuttings in jars of water on her windowsill, and starting off new spider plants by pegging their plantlets into a circle of smaller pots around the mother plant – holding them in place with one of her hairpins. She gave potfuls to friends and church bazaars, progeny of the monster that sat on the what-not a few feet back from the windowsill – the windowsill that was really a miniature green-house, where the light squinted through, dappled by the leaves of her flourishing jungle.

On the other side of us, in the top house of our lump of terrace, a Scottish family lived for a short while, to be replaced by the Dinsdales and their ever-expanding brood. The Dinsdales had married in their teens, to sharp intakes of breath and sideways glances from the neighbours. Their children were still arriving long after I'd left home. Gerry – bearded and with the suntanned torso of a Greek god when he dug his vegetable patch – was the best whistler in the town. You could hear him coming from the top of the street. He used to lean out of his upstairs toilet window with an airgun to shoot the sparrows that ate his peas. Mum wasn't happy about this and she complained to my father: 'Alan, tell him off. He'll have somebody's eye out.' He never did.

I watched from the comfort of my sister's bedroom window; in awe of his prowess with the gun, but saddened at the sight of the little grey-and-brown birds toppling off the gutter of his garden shed and landing with a puff of dust on the sun-baked earth below. Half of me wanted to have a go myself; the other half wanted to snatch the airgun from him.

Gerry would join in with our games sometimes – kicking a ball about or generally being silly. The other parents in the street were a bit sniffy about this and thought he should grow up. We were glad that he didn't.

Winnie, his wife, had one of the loudest voices I've ever heard and was inordinately fond of the word 'bugger'. But my mother (who never swore, except to repeat what somebody else had said, which she did with some relish) said she had a good heart.

Beyond the top house of our terrace, the back cut through to the front, bordered by a high stone wall. On the other side of it lived the Forrests and their children – a Catholic family – he a joiner, whose brother owned the local removal firm, she a housewife with a sing-song voice and a capacity to burst into tears at the most minor of domestic misfortunes. I listened time without number as a hysterical Mrs Forrest, sounding like an operatic heroine in full flood, regaled me at breakneck speed with the disaster that had befallen her daughter Philomena on that particular day. I never understood a word of it – so fast did the words come, and in such a high-pitched coloratura – and then she'd rush back indoors, wringing her hands in her pinny all the while, slam the door, and shriek up the stairs to some child to come down and have its tea, or shut up and get into bed. The air had a spectacular stillness when Mrs Forrest's voice died away.

The high spot of Tommy Forrest's life was when he met the Pope. A neighbour pointed to a photo of the two of them in the *Ilkley Gazette* and asked, 'Who's that with Tommy Forrest?'

Across from us were the Hudsons and the Feathers, the Gells and the Phillipses and, in the middle house, Mr Smith, the chimney sweep, who smoked a pipe and had a gold watch chain.

It was in the road between the hosues that we played most of the time: me and Mickey Hudson, Stephen Feather and Robert Petty, Ralph Clayton and 'Dokey' Gell. His name was Donald, but everybody called him 'Dokey'. He was older than the rest of us, and quickly grew out of our childish games – kick-can, a livelier version of hide-and-seek; cricket with the wicket chalked on the bus-garage wall; and football with only one goal.

There was little danger from passing cars – nobody had one. Not until my dad got his van when I was nine or ten. Dennis Petty, the coalman, had a lorry, and Stanley Hudson had his greengrocer's van, but they were hardly ever in evidence.

Nothing much happened in our street. At least, nothing out of the ordinary.

Early memories are deceptive and sometimes triggered by photographs, so that you kid yourself you can remember a particular event that exists only in a faded snapshot. Which may be why I think I can remember my grandfather walking me, aged about one and a half, between the rows of sweet peas on his allotment down by the river. He is dressed in his waistcoat and trilby, with a tie, and there are silvery lids of Cadbury's cocoa tins dangling on strings to frighten away the sparrows. I am dressed in baggy bloomers and a bit of a girly top. But I can see the rest of that allotment in my mind's eye . . .

The Allotments

I t never occurred to me when I was little that allotments were anything less than glamorous places. Grandad Hardisty's was not situated in some grimy city backwater – a piece of reclaimed waste ground. Instead, it was on the south bank of the River Wharfe, and sloped gently down towards the water. You couldn't reach the river with your watering can – there was a fence and a pathway in between – but you could hear the sound of water, and of the birds that sang in the weeping willows that towered over the bank and dangled their feathery wands into the slow-moving current. If you raised your eyes and looked up from the water, you could see Middleton Woods and, beyond them, one or two red-tiled house roofs peeping through the trees. A blissful spot. A happy spot. I imagined that all allotments were like this – places of escape, places of peace and solitude.

Grandad's plot was nothing out of the ordinary when it came to features. He had nothing as grand as a greenhouse, like some of the others. Not that they had proper 'bought' greenhouses with pitched roofs. The greenhouses on the allotments were cobbled together from old window frames. The flat roof would have a gentle slope in one direction so that it could shed the rain, and there would be some sort of fabricated door on rusty hinges to allow access. An old oil drum would be propped up on lumps of flagstone at one corner to catch the rain. If you were lucky, one of the windows would open to allow ventilation; if it did not, then you opened the door, or you cooked in summer, along with your tomatoes. In Yorkshire in the 1950s, no one grew tomatoes outside; they'd have perished in the chilly air if they'd been planted before mid-June, and with the frosts coming in September that didn't give you much time to mature the crop. No, tomatoes were greenhouse plants, and being of such a tender and snooty disposition, were probably a bit scornful of the structures on the allotments that the owners were pleased to call greenhouses.

Patches of polythene would be tacked in place where a carelessly wielded spade had smashed a pane of glass, and none of the window frames would be the same colour. It seemed that they were a hotch-potch of three shades of Brolac – white, cream and 'council-house green'.

These little crystal palaces were Heath Robinson attempts at protected cultivation, and the sheds were generally of the same sort of design, though one or two of them had the luxury of a veranda – courtesy of old floorboards and some barley-twist banisters that had been pulled out of a house that was going 'contemporary'.

Mr Emmett had the plot next door to Grandad. He was a dour man with a flat cap and horn-rimmed glasses and a face that seemed to be permanently folded. If you said hello to him, he'd grunt, but he'd never look up.

He seemed only to grow vegetables that were as serious as he was – long-maturing root crops like parsnips and swedes, savoy cabbages and red cabbages and beetroots. There was never anything as frivolous as a lettuce or a spring onion, and Mr Emmett never seemed to evince any pleasure in harvesting anything, even when he was cycling home with his vegetables propped on the handlebars.

Grandad's allotment was different. It was friendly, like he was – an allotment that as well as growing vegetables for the pot, grew a few flowers for Grandma to put in a cut-glass vase in the front room: pale-blue scabious, pink and white sweet williams and long rows of sweet peas trained up rows of beanpoles.

At the bottom end of the patch were three or four old brass bedsteads fastened with twisted wire to lengths of rusty angle-iron that had been hammered into the soil as posts. Over them were trained the spiny stems of blackberries – their fruits could be pressed into your mouth by the fistful if you could avoid the tiny thorns that become impossible to remove once bedded in the soft skin of your

fingers. I learned, early on, to pick them carefully, and to try not to stain my clothes for fear of a slap on the back of the legs from my mum. I'd pull the four corners of my hanky together (I think I was born with one in my left-hand trouser pocket) to make a bag, and drop them in it. Their juice would come through and stain the white cotton, but she didn't mind too much about that. As allotment features go, there are few that are more decorative than a row of blackberries trained over brass bedsteads – the knobs poking through and gleaming gold in the summer sun.

A tiny shed, no bigger than a sentry box, stood in one corner of the plot, leaning downhill, and in it were Grandad's tools, all stacked in a corner – a rake with a wobbly head, several types of hoe with rusty blades, a spade and a fork and a heavy pair of shears with wooden handles. There were other tools, too, that I never saw him use, and a rusty cobbler's last – I thought it was probably there in case he needed to make a running repair to the black boots he always wore, but most often it was used to prop open the peeling door that had a habit of closing of its own accord and trapping your fingers when you weren't looking.

There were spilled seeds on the dusty floor – biscuit-brown beans and the blue-grey beads of cabbages. The granules of Growmore that leaked from the dampened lower corner of a paper sack leaning in the opposite corner filled the air with their acrid tang. He scattered it between the cabbages and cauliflowers every now and again, having decanted it into an old galvanised bucket. With his black trilby pushed back on his head and his pipeful of Condor sticking out from under his walrus moustache, he'd become the personification of the hymn, and I'd hum to myself as I watched him scattering the feed among his crops – 'We plough the fields and scatter the good seed on the land.' It didn't matter that it was Growmore, not seeds, that he was scattering; the sentiments were still appropriate, and thanks to Grandad's almighty hand, as well as God's, we never seemed to be short of vegetables in our kitchen.

A long row of rhubarb ran alongside the blackberries, and there were rows and rows of savoy cabbages whose corrugated leaves of rubbery leather were dappled with soot. The soot was mixed with water in an old washing copper sunk into the ground by the rhubarb row and sprayed on to the cabbages, cauliflowers and Brussels sprouts with a long brass syringe to deter caterpillars. It had to be scrubbed off before the crops were in any way edible, but it did keep off the caterpillars. It probably helped to build up our antibodies into the bargain.

If you ever complained to Grandad about the blackened state of his greens, he'd shake his head and say, 'Tha'll eat more than a peck a muck afore tha dees.'

On sunny Saturday afternoons I'd be wheeled down to the allotment in my pram or my pushchair, and from under the sunshade I could squint at Grandad and my dad as they turned over the soil together. In later years I'd sit on the grey plank bench by the shed, tucking into an egg sandwich – they were always egg – and a glass of pop while they did the heavy work.

Grandad was always the boss; Dad the helpful, if reluctantly press-ganged, son-in-law.

'When tha gets to't'end o't'row, will tha move t'line?'

'Are we doin' another row, then?' my dad would ask wearily.

'Aye. Then we'll go to't'club for a pint.'

The pint of Tetley's in the Liberal Club would be the carrot, and while I sat outside on the wall, drinking a glass of orange squash and eating a custard cream, the two men would risk a quick game of dominoes before saying goodbye and making their separate ways home.

Dad never liked gardening, but home-grown vegetables saved a few bob. He took over the allotment after Grandad died, planting cabbages and showing me how to 'puddle them in', and earthing up long rows of potatoes. But his heart wasn't in it and he finally gave it up, confining his attempts at vegetable gardening to a few desultory rows of blue-green Brussels sprouts in the back garden. There was a smile on his face when even that patch was put down to grass and Mum planted a hydrangea instead.

We lived, for the first year of my life – the bit I can't remember – with my paternal grandmother, Florrie Titchmarsh, at 9 Dean Street, a tiny two-up, two-down terraced house with an attic. It was a tricky time. My father's mother was not an easy woman to get on with – bird-like and hard to please – a state of affairs not improved by the fact that my father's spinster sister, Auntie Alice, frequently took to her bed with some ailment or other, which was known within the family as 'idleitis'. For years I assumed this was a legitimate complaint. During the time when Mum and Dad lived with the in-laws, Auntie Alice was billeted with the lady she used to clean for – Mrs Heap – up the posh end of town. She would come round to Dean Street for meals, and to offer the benefit of her advice, which was usually based on hearsay or the homespun wisdom of her friend Phyllis Lupton rather than personal experience. Auntie Alice hadn't had much of that.

Grandma Titch and Auntie Alice

I t was a sort of double act – Grandma Titch and Auntie Alice – a bit like bacon and eggs, accident and emergency, or Morecambe and Wise. Except that they weren't that funny. Well, not as reliably, though they did have their moments. If you'd have asked me as a child, I'd have said that they hated one another, though I suppose they had the same relationship as any mother and daughter living together – contempt born of familiarity.

When I was born, Auntie Alice would have been forty and Grandma sixty-two. They were still living together when Grandma died at the age of ninety, and still arguing.

To be fair to Grandma Titch, Auntie Alice must have been a bit of a pain. While Grandma worked like a Trojan from dawn till dusk, Auntie Alice would find any possible excuse to take to her bed with her nerves or 'one of my heads'.

Sometimes I'd have to take her up a cup of tea during one of her confinements.

'Take this up to your Auntie Alice, will you?' Grandma would ask. 'I've lost patience.'

I'd tap gingerly on the back bedroom door. There would be no reply to the first knock. Ever. Then I'd tap again, a little bit louder. That was the cue for a muffled groan. At the third knock, a weak 'Come in' would issue from beneath the blankets and I'd go into the darkened, airless room with the cup of strong, sugary tea, to be engulfed by the sweet-and-sour smell of spinster invalidity.

Auntie Alice's room always smelled like this. The window was never open, and the atmosphere was one that owed its complexity to

31

a mixture of Germolene and stale talcum powder, boxes of Milk Tray and bedsocks.

'How are you?' I'd venture, trying not to breathe too deeply.

'Not very well, luv,' would come, muffled, from somewhere beneath the quilted floral eiderdown. It was too dark for me to be able to make out more than the vague form of a portly supine body.

As a child trained to be jolly even in times of discomfort (often to the irritation of others), I could never understand how Auntie Alice could be so ungrateful to someone – anyone – who'd climbed the stairs to bring her a cup of tea.

I'd try to be optimistic. 'Are you any better than yesterday?'

'Not really, no. Your auntie Alice is a very poorly lady.'

'Oh.' I didn't feel there was much of an answer to that.

The room was tiny. Just a single bed along one wall, a wardrobe and a dressing table with a chair. The wallpaper was one of faded flowers. A bit like Auntie Alice. There was barely room to walk around, and the only thing that would catch your eye would be the gleaming rim of the chamber pot underneath the bed.

'Bye, then.' I prayed that I'd get out of the door before the dreaded request was made. I usually prayed in vain.

Auntie Alice raised her head from the pillow a fraction of an inch, her curly hair encased in a thick net, designed to keep it in place in case she met anybody important the following day. 'Could you empty the article?'

My heart sank. 'Righto.'

I felt under the bed for the chamber pot and carried it carefully at arm's length out of the door and downstairs to the backyard, trying not to look at the contents. Grandma and Auntie Alice only had an outside lavatory, and if you were taken short in the middle of the night, you had to resort to the portable version.

Right up to her death in the 1970s Grandma never had an inside lavatory or a bathroom. Once a week the galvanised tin bath would be lifted from its nail in the coalhouse at the end of the backyard and set up in front of the fire. Hot water from the gas geyser in the kitchen would be ferried to it in a large saucepan, and Grandma would wash herself all over with a flannel and a bar of Fairy soap.

Once our own bath was installed when we moved to Nelson Road, she'd visit us once a week to conduct her ablutions in more savoury surroundings, and the tin bath was left to gather coal dust in the shed.

Occasionally I would stay the night with Grandma when Mum and Dad were going out and couldn't get a babysitter. I'd sleep on a camp bed rigged up in a corner of her room, and if I happened to be awake in the middle of the night, I would hear her relieving herself into the potty by the side of the bed. I pretended to be asleep while she rearranged her nightie and pushed 'the article', as both she and her daughter always called it, back under her bed. Sometimes I could hear Auntie Alice snoring in the back bedroom next door.

Auntie Alice had always been a bit fragile. My mum blamed it on something called the Oxford Movement – a religious body active in her youth who were bent on moral rearmament. Rather than gaining anything from her involvement, it seemed that Auntie Alice's armoury had been sadly depleted. She spent the rest of her life in bits.

But she was a good soul. She saved threepence a week for me and my sister and our two cousins all her life, and gave us the proceeds twice a year. That was undeniably useful – a lump sum, rather than a few pennies that would soon disappear on six ha'penny chews or a lucky bag. With several shillings I could buy seeds. Or Airfix kits. Or bits for my bike.

Grandma herself was besotted by bingo, especially on her annual week's holiday in Morecambe. She seemed exceptionally lucky, and would usually come back with an extra bag filled with her prizes. They were, without exception, things that no one could get excited about – a tartan umbrella made of cotton (not waterproof), a watch with luminous numbers but not luminous hands, an assortment of tin trays and the two basic prizes that always went down well in Morecambe – pac-a-macs and plastic rainhoods. At the time of her death Grandma had enough rainhoods in her sideboard to cover the heads of every pensioner in Ilkley. The more interesting of these prizes (and that wasn't saying much) often found their way underneath our Christmas tree. My mother was not impressed.

Auntie Alice was also a bingo fan and seldom missed a whist drive or a beetle drive, always in the company of Phyllis Lupton. They made a curious pair: Auntie Alice, plump and cylindrical in a tight floral-patterned crimplene dress and cardy, and over them a camel coat with a belt round the middle that made her look like a parcel. Phyllis, by then in her sixties, her face running W. H. Auden a close second in the wrinkle stakes, would be heavily powdered, rouged and lipsticked, and her body draped in a fake leopard-skin coat – the short, belt-less kind shaped like a bell that Hollywood starlets would wear. The two of them would totter up the road to the Church Institute, where they'd install themselves at their favourite table, and for the rest of the evening Phyllis would chain-smoke her Woodbines and Auntie Alice might risk a port and lemon. They usually did well, but always grumbled about some rival's good fortune: 'That Dorothy Hunnebell – you'd think she'd give up after winning twice, wouldn't you, and give the rest of us a chance?'

'She went to Otley last week. To the Mechanics Institute. Won the jackpot. Twenty pounds,' complained Auntie Alice.

'Don't you worry, love,' consoled Phyllis. 'She'll have no luck.'

The effect that the chance of winning any prize would have on Auntie Alice was astonishing. Whenever a party was in prospect – be it a family get-together or something organised by the church at the institute – Auntie Alice would be at the front of the queue. Grown men would give her the benefit of the doubt in musical chairs. They didn't need to. When the music stopped, she could have her bottom on the bentwood before the fittest of them had so much as crooked their knees. Then she'd laugh sheepishly in that fey little way she had as they retired to the side of the room, and make a great show of heaving herself up to the vertical and tottering round the room once more to the strains of 'Country Gardens'. At bingo and musical chairs, Auntie Alice's reputation was Olympian.

When she wasn't pursuing the glittering prizes, or cleaning for Mrs Heap, or so poorly that she took herself off to bed, she'd sit in front of the gas fire with a mug of tea, gazing into the flames until her legs were mottled maroon. Her hands would always shake when she lifted the cup to her mouth, or when she tried to get change out of her purse. I don't know why; aside from the odd port and lemon, she was never one for the bottle.

There was never a man in Auntie Alice's life, at least not that I ever knew of. She probably hadn't the energy. Instead, she just dreamed. 'I wish I could play like that,' she remarked on seeing Russ Conway fingering the ivories on *The Billy Cotton Band Show*.

'Well, you could have done if you'd practised,' came Grandma's dismissive retort.

Grandma was not a sitter. She was a doer. She'd be out working or shopping or driving my mum demented by turning up on our back doorstep just as tea was being served.

'That looks nice,' she'd say, leaning against the door frame as the MacRae kipper fillets were being served. My mum was never one for large portions – a single pack of fillets along with some mashed potato would be made to feed the four of us. Mum would be at the far end of the breakfast bar by the coke boiler where it was warmest, then me, then my sister, then Dad nearest the back door. Mum would sigh and take a bit off each plate, and Grandma would perch on a buffet and eat her portion, chattering all the while. We none of us grew very large.

We had only one meal a year at Grandma's and that would be on Boxing Day. It was not something that we looked forward to as children, not least because both Mum and Dad used to dread it. Mum would feel she was being got at the whole time, and Dad would know that she'd be in a right state by the time we got home and bend his ear something rotten.

We'd turn up at about four o'clock in the afternoon to find that Grandma's front room had been rearranged so that the lumpy black and grey sofa and the two hard-backed wing chairs were pushed against the walls and the gate-leg dining table was fully extended in the centre. It would be covered in green baize, topped with a white damask cloth that had seen better days. Set upon it would be a large pork pie, bowls of pickled onions and unidentifiable chutneys, plates of bread and butter, boiled potatoes and a small and particularly dry lump of boiled ham. The Ty-phoo tea in the brown pot would be eye-wateringly strong, and the mince pies that followed would be hard and dry. It wasn't that Grandma was inhospitable; it was simply that she was unaware of the nature of her produce. Maybe after a lifetime of serving food, she'd ceased to notice what it looked like or to exercise any form of quality control.

The air would be cold – the gas fire was small, even for a room of this size, and the blanket-like curtain fastened over the front door was not especially effective at keeping out the draught. The smiling, battered paper moon that hung over it would be blowing in the wind all evening.

'Come on now, eat up. Alice! Is that kettle boiled yet?'

'Course it's not. I've only just put it on . . .'

'Well, get yourself framed. I don't know why it takes you so much longer than it takes me.'

'You can do it yourself if you think you can do it any faster.'

Grandma would bustle into the kitchen. 'Well, I'm not surprised – the gas has gone out. Did you put the money in the meter?'

'How was I to know we'd run out?' would be the baleful reply.

'Well, couldn't you hear it?'

Grandma would bustle back, muttering under her breath, and go to a box on the sideboard for a fistful of pennies. 'Here you are, Alan,' she'd say to me. 'Put them in the meter.'

I'd leave the table and open the low cupboard in the corner of the room – the damp-smelling one where the broken clockwork train and the toy polar bear with one eye were kept – and feed the pennies into the grey meter, turning the handle until each one dropped into the bottom of the metal box. The gas would once more leap into life with a hiss and Grandma would snap through the open kitchen doorway, 'Alice! It's on again. Light the cooker or there'll be an accident.'

Poor Auntie Alice. She seemed resigned to the fact that she was Grandma's scapegoat, ever ready to cope with vented spleen and to take the blame for whatever might go wrong. Every family had an 'Auntie Alice' back then – the sort of disappointed elderly spinster that Noël Coward epitomised in one of his songs: 'We must all be very kind to Auntie Jessie, she's never been a mother or a wife. It's unkind to throw your toys at her or make a vulgar noise at her, she hasn't had a very happy life.'

Maiden aunts were as much a part of family life as grandparents, and could be relied on to indulge their nieces and nephews. After all, as mothers would sometimes unkindly remark, they had nothing else to spend their money on. They fulfilled their role as the butt of family jokes, handy babysitters in emergencies and martyrs to ill health.

By way of consoling herself in her position, Auntie Alice decided one day to have a cat. She brought home a tabby kitten from some friend of Mrs Heap's, and I was allowed to give it a name. I decided on Penelope – the name of a rather nice-looking girl with dark and glossy plaits in a book I was reading at the time. 'Penny' she became, but, like Auntie Alice, she was not destined for a happy life. When she was two years old, she was kicked in the teeth by some young tearaways and, subsequently, her mouth went up at one side and down at the other, giving her an everlasting expression of disappointment. A bit like Auntie Alice.

And yet, somehow, Auntie Alice seemed to accept her position in the family pecking order, probably because she never saw herself as we saw her. In her own eyes, she was an independent woman who just happened to live with her mother. I don't think we ever gave her credit for the fact that she had a mind of her own, probably because she rarely brought it into play. Certainly not in our eyes. She was always an also-ran, an appendage to Grandma, and on Boxing Day she was treated like a maid, forever being exhorted to get up from the table and bring in more hot water, or more cake, or a slab of rock-hard butter from the cold, damp larder next to the scullery.

Once enough of the food had been eaten to satisfy Grandma's sense of hospitality, and as much of the full-strength tea as possible had been drunk, the washing-up would be done, the table folded away, and the chairs rearranged in a circle for the Christmas games that would complete the evening's entertainment – I Packed My Trunk and I Spy were as adventurous as it got.

There was no escape until the Christmas cake and cheese had done its rounds – cake of unsurpassed density and Cheddar cheese so strong it made your eyes water – but, with any luck, by the time it got to half past eight Mum and Dad would be able to excuse themselves on account of their children's tiredness, and after a prickly kiss from Grandma and a damp one from Auntie Alice, we'd wend our weary way home with profound relief. It was all over for another year, and sharing our kipper fillets with Grandma did seem, on the whole, to be less of an ordeal than sharing her Boxing Day tea.

Dad's brother, Uncle Jim, worked at Moisley's shoe shop on the Grove, and his wife, Auntie Jenny, was always held up as a paragon of virtue by Grandma Titchmarsh. This, in itself, might have been borne by my mother, had Auntie Jenny not committed the cardinal sin of being born a Geordie. Mum couldn't stand Geordies. 'They think they know everything,' she'd mutter. Grandma herself, being from Beverley – further north than Ilkley – probably felt a greater affinity with Jenny than with Mum, and she wasn't backward at coming forward about Jenny's latest exploits: 'Our Jenny's got a new coat. A lovely camel one. Got it in Brown Muffs. Bought mind. Not homemade.'

Me Mam

'M e mam' was always the most beautiful woman in the world. The yardstick by which other women's beauty was measured. Not Hollywood film stars – they were different, unreal – but when it came to local women, I accepted that my mother was the best-looking of them all. A bit like the Queen. Mum and the Queen seemed to have everything – grace, poise and nice clothes – and they were both always right. The Queen was always right because she was the Queen, and my mum was always right because she said so. It never occurred to me that occasionally there might be a different point of view.

It seemed, back then, that between them my mum and dad could do everything. Dad was good with his hands – a plumber by trade, he was skilled at home improvements – and Mum made everything that she and her children wore, apart from our St Michael knickers and socks, and the Clark's shoes.

First there were little check shirts and grey flannel shorts. Not for me the embarrassing kind worn by some boys at school. The sort you had to grow into. The sort that were too long and came down to your knees. The sort that were of really rough flannel and seemed to develop unsavoury-looking yellow patches in unfortunate places. No, mine always finished a respectable three inches above the knee and fitted around the waist, thanks to a lump of elastic that, somehow, Mum had managed to conceal within the material.

Most Saturdays would involve a trip to the Remnant Shop in Leeds Road for some kind of fabric, unwound from its flattened roll with a satisfying thud on the smooth counter with its inbuilt brass ruler. Huge black-handled scissors would be used to nick the edge of the fabric, which would then be rent across by the lady behind the counter, and folded up and slipped into a brown paper bag.

With the material stowed in her shopping basket, Mum would take my hand and walk me from Leeds Road up to Railway Road and the tiny haberdasher's shop next door to the Essoldo Cinema. In part of its grandiose white-tiled frontage, with the pink neon 'Essoldo' motif shining out towards the moors, was Kell's, where Miss MacEvoy dispensed buttons and bias binding, knicker elastic and press studs – everything for the home dressmaker.

Miss Mac was a round little lady with a bob of white hair. She wore Perspex-framed glasses and was always eating.

'Hello, Miss Mac, we're looking for some buttons to go with this,' and Mum would pull out the edge of the fabric to be met with a sharp intake of breath from Miss Mac. Always.

'Ooh, that's tricky. I'm not sure I've anything . . .' she'd say as she screwed up her eyes and scrutinised the glazed cotton, the poplin or the floral print.

The wall behind her, on the other side of the counter, was covered from floor to ceiling with brown wooden drawers of varying sizes. Some had glazed fronts that showed off their contents; others bore labels: 'Brass buttons, various', 'Hooks and eyes', 'Zips 6 in', 'Zips 12 in' and 'Bodkins, pins and needles'.

It was hard to believe that somewhere in this Aladdin's cave, Miss Mac did not have something that would suit. And she did. Always.

'I might just have . . .' Her words would trail away as she got out the small wooden stepladder, opened it out and then climbed to the top row of drawers, where she teetered precariously, opening this one and that, occasionally with a disappointed grunt, until with a cry of triumph, 'Aha! There you are. I thought so,' she'd make her way down, to my mother's relief, without coming a cropper.

The buttons would be dropped into a small brown paper bag, and change given from a large wooden drawer that opened with a bright 'ping', and we'd leave Miss Mac to go on eating whatever it was that we had interrupted.

Wool came from the Co-op drapery store on the corner of Leeds Road and Little Lane. Here, Mr Hay presided – a tall, quiet, bald man who sold wool by the skein. We had to make it into balls ourselves – me with my hands held out wide, and Mum winding away until I felt that my arms would fall off. 'Only three more to go, Sparrow, then you can go out.'

The hand-knitted jumpers were V-necked to start with, in safe colours – fawn or light grey. Then she knitted me a royal-blue one. A few years later the knitting needles were laid aside and she bought a machine that was capable of creating the most elaborate Fair Isle patterns; not the sort of thing in which you could melt into the background – at that time infinitely preferable to being noticed.

There was a camel coat, double-breasted with wide lapels and collar and a belt; the buttons were round and leathery. It was worn for best on Sundays, with a peaked cap and woollen mittens, when we walked down by the river, or up on the moors.

In spare moments she'd knock up a scarf or a balaclava helmet – the latter essential in winter after someone threw a snowball at me and caused an abscess on my neck. At least, that's what Mum put it down to. 'I'm not having you getting another abscess. If there's going to be any snowball throwing, you wear your balaclava.' I hated it.

Then there would be the thin white cotton tape (bought from Miss Mac) that was sewn on to my mittens and led up through the arms of my coat. Other kids were allowed to lose their mittens – you could see them stuck individually on the tops of iron railings on snowy days – but not me.

Mum would write her own version of Cash's name tapes with black indelible ink on little strips of the white cotton tape, to be sewn into the back of any garment that might be confused with somebody else's at school. Not that they ever were. Mum's clothing was in a class of its own and never contained any labels other than her own.

But her *pièces de résistance* were her dresses. My father was a part-time fireman as well as being a plumber, and once a year the firemen would have a dance in the room above the fire station, or there might be a dance in the King's Hall that they'd go to for a treat. A new dress would have to be made especially for the occasion.

There was a peachy-pink brocade number with a full skirt; a large brown-and-white floral-print dress with a hemline that was narrower than usual with a big bow at the front of the skirt – we called it her 'tulip' dress; and eventually a gold lamé two-piece suit that was simply the last word in glamour. I peered over the back of the settee open-mouthed as Dad led her out through the front door, glittering under the light of the street lamp.

Sometimes she'd pack one of her special dresses for our annual holiday, and she and Dad would waltz round the Tower Ballroom at Blackpool like Fred Astaire and Ginger Rogers. They moved as one. Mum always seemed to know just where Dad was going to step next; it was a mystery I could not fathom. He never seemed to say anything to her that might give her a clue as to his next move, and yet she knew instinctively when to step backwards or forwards.

I noticed her hand on his shoulder. It did not grip it, like the hands of most women on the floor; instead, she only lightly touched him with the back of her hand, her palm facing outwards. It seemed supremely elegant.

The contrast presented by my father's appearance in his suit, compared with his working clothes of dark-blue bib-and-brace overalls, boots and flat cap, could not have been greater. Here he was, with his shiny Vaselined hair (he said he preferred it to Brylcreem as it didn't smell so sickly) gliding round the polished wooden floor, doing those showy quicksteps with a calm, imperturbable expression on his face. Occasionally they would make eye contact and smile knowingly at each other, all the while seemingly oblivious to the other couples around them. Their minds seemed to be somewhere else, and then when the music stopped, Dad would take Mum's hand and lead her back to the seats round the ballroom with hardly a change of expression. 'Cup of tea, Beff?'

'That'd be nice.'

Back at home, the dress would be hung in the wardrobe once more, and Mum would spend her days in a skirt and cardigan. She never wore trousers until I was eleven. She'd been a bit restless all day, having come back from the shops with a brown paper parcel that she took straight up to her bedroom. Then she came down and made a cup of tea, but she couldn't settle.

Eventually she got up quite quickly, went to her bedroom and closed the door. I was worried. What could it be? Was she not feeling well? Was something wrong between her and Dad? I went up to my room, but as I got to the top of the stairs, the door of her bedroom opened to reveal her standing there in a pair of neatly tailored trousers. They were of fawn cotton, and finished about six inches above her ankle – the sort of flattering cut that was fashionable in the fifties.

'Wow!' I could not stop myself. She looked sensational.

That was all it took. She closed the bedroom door smartly and disappeared. Ten minutes later she came back downstairs in the skirt and cardigan. It would be another few weeks before she would try the trousers on again, and after that they became her daily uniform.

My mother always had a dislike of hospitals, and whenever anyone was admitted, she would do her level best to avoid visiting them. It was not that she was inconsiderate, neither was it simply the fact that she was impatient with ill health. Her experiences in hospital had always been unhappy ones, which is strange considering that throughout her life there was only one way you could get my mother to do something she didn't want to do, and that was to get the doctor to suggest it to her.

Doctors and Nurses

To watch Dr Senior jump out of his little red MG sports car was one of the high spots of my mother's life. 'He was very dashing,' she'd say, wistfully, with a look that could have given Celia Johnson a run for her money in *Brief Encounter*. By the time I came along, Dr Senior had an MG saloon and a bit of a stoop, but he retained the deep voice, the Oxford accent, the pipe clamped between his teeth and my mother's admiration.

The reason that we played doctors and nurses on the old bed frames down in the junk yard by the saleroom probably had something to do with the high regard in which Mum held doctors. Come to think of it, it wasn't just doctors. It was most men.

Mum was always happier in their company than in the company of women. She did have a 'hen night' once a week with three friends she had known since the early days of her marriage – they'd meet at each other's houses to chat and knit and have a bit of supper – but on the whole women irritated her and she did not seek out their company. 'Why would I want to join the WI? All they do is argue over the teapot.'

It was not that she was unhappy in her marriage – she doted on my father – but she loved to flirt, and to have men make a fuss of her, even later in life with some of my college mates who were half her age. It made her feel good. Made her feel like a woman. And, to be perfectly honest, I think she regarded other women as competition.

I'm quite sure that Dr Senior was unaware of the effect he had on her, or that she was more impressed with members of the medical profession than of any other. Among the working classes 'Doctor's' word was regarded as law. He was never called 'the doctor'. The definite article was dropped as if to emphasise his authority. He was 'Doctor'. Like 'God'.

Doctors were from another walk of life altogether. A better class of person. We knew of no one whose son or daughter had become a doctor; the position was unattainable except by birth, as far as Mum was concerned.

She also had great admiration for Dr Senior's personal hygiene. 'He always has such clean hands, for a smoker.'

I don't think the remark was directed at my dad – then a ten-a-day Senior Service man. It was more of a quiet reflection. But I can remember, myself, the smell of Dr Senior, and in spite of the fact that he smoked a pipe, he always smelled of tweed and a sort of classy disinfectant. His hands and stethoscope were deathly cold, and he had a posh accent.

Grandma and Auntie Alice would compare notes about the different treatments that doctors within the same practice had prescribed. There was Dr Ferris, Dr Armstrong, Dr Senior and Dr Gott, as well as the kindly female Dr Hillis, who wore her grey hair pinned up behind and always looked highly intelligent. My mother's feeling towards her, being a well-spoken woman in a man's profession, was bordering on awe.

If Auntie Alice had a particular problem, then Grandma would say, 'Well, you want to get yourself along to Dr Ferris and get him to give you some of those tablets he gave Florence Grange. They sorted her out.'

It mattered not whether Auntie Alice's complaint was the same as that of her friend Florence Grange; Grandma was convinced that Auntie Alice never asked for the right tablets or ointment. Why else would she always be ill?

My mother was equally impatient of illness, and as a child, the only way I could be guaranteed to be allowed to stay at home was if I had actually been physically sick. Even then it was probably the prospect of embarrassment at me throwing up in the classroom that made her keep me at home, rather than the belief that it would help me get better more quickly.

As with all children, there were days when I did not want to go in.

Days when I just felt a bit ropey, or days when I was being picked on and couldn't face the thought of another day of mickey-taking; another day of gritting my teeth and getting on with it. I don't suppose I was any more feeble than anybody else; just too sensitive for my own good.

But 'feeling a bit poorly' was not enough, so on days when I really wanted a result, I would go to the bathroom, close the door, and make retching noises, hopefully loud enough for my mother to hear. Then I'd come out and do my best to look pale.

I did once consider tipping the contents of a tin of vegetable soup into the washbasin, but in the end I thought that might be going a bit far, and if Mum had found the empty tin, she might have put two and two together. It was not worth the risk. Generally, if I *said* I had been sick, she would believe me, and by the middle of the afternoon I would have improved and she would satisfy herself that she had done the right thing.

Sometimes there were health scares. In the early 1960s the prospect of a smallpox outbreak seemed a real possibility, and so all parents and children were summoned to the outpatients of the Coronation Hospital to be vaccinated. The queue stretched for half a mile down the road. Nobody seemed to mind, and families stood chatting at the side of the road, shuffling forward obediently and with good grace as the queue shortened, until eventually they were ushered into the curtained cubicles and attacked with the hypodermic by one of the local GPs. Drs Senior, Armstrong, Ferris, Gott and Hillis had turned out in force to man the needles. There was great community spirit about the whole thing.

The abscess that my mother claimed I got as a result of a snowball hitting my neck led to a short stay in hospital. I don't remember much, other than seeing screens being pulled around me while the wound was being dressed and slivers of soggy skin being removed with forceps and placed in an enamel kidney-shaped dish. But I remember breaking my leg, not least because it coincided with the death of my mother's parents.

I feel guilty now for loving my mother's parents more than I loved my dad's mum. Grandma Titch was a tough old bird — she had to be, with a husband dying relatively young and a sickly daughter often confined to the back bedroom — but she was good-hearted, and mellowed a lot in old age. In her eighties the tough and prickly-lipped busybody transformed into a benign old lady with a ready smile. She'd say, as she ran her fingers through my hair every time I returned home and went to see her, 'Do you know, I'm sure you're getting darker.' You had to warm to her.

But Grandma and Grandad Hardisty were every child's idea of what grandparents should be. They looked like them, sounded like them and acted like them, and my feelings towards them, at the age of six or seven, were little short of adoration.

Grandma and Grandad Hardisty

G randma and Grandad Hardisty lived in Ash Grove, a street that ran parallel with the river. Grandad was a ganger for the council highways department – a sort of foreman – and cultivated his allotment in his spare time. He was everything a grandad should be – right down to the walrus moustache and the black trilby. Grandma Hardisty was tall and thin, with horn-rimmed spectacles and floral aprons. They were a devoted couple.

Grandad would sit by the black range in the kitchen, slurping tea out of his saucer and smoking pipefuls of Condor tobacco, while Grandma baked biscuits in the oven next to the fire, and spooned sugar into her husband's tea from an amber sugar bowl.

They had two sets of boy-girl twins – Auntie Barbara (Bee) whose twin Charles had died on St Patrick's Day when he was only six weeks old, and my mum, Bessie, and her brother, George Herbert (Bert). Between Mum and Uncle Bert there was always a sense of unspoken rivalry. They were not as close as many twins; their temperaments were probably too similar to make for easy relations.

Auntie Bee lived with her husband, Uncle Herbert – a grumpy greengrocer – in Otley; Uncle Bert – a happier grocer – lived in Burley-in-Wharfedale with Auntie Edie, the daughter of the game-keeper from Denton, a tiny hamlet on the hillside between Burley-in-Wharfedale and Ilkley. Each couple had two children. Most of the time they all got on reasonably well, though there were the usual family tensions.

But Grandma and Grandad Hardisty were loved by their children

55

and grandchildren alike, and every now and again some example of Grandad's sentimentality would manifest itself, either in the form of the tulips, sweet williams and wallflowers that he grew alongside the path to their front door to scent the air in May or in the singing of a song.

'We've been together now for forty years, and it don't seem a day too much—'

'Shut up, Herbert!' my grandmother would admonish.

'There ain't a lady living in the land that I'd swap for me dear old Dutch!'

'Daft beggar!' she'd say softly, then wipe away a tear with the corner of her pinny.

They did everything together, right to the end.

I was eight when I broke my leg. The year was 1957. It was nothing spectacular. Someone stuck out their leg in the playground and I tripped over it. I was scooped up by Mr Wall, a teacher who wore brown tweed suits and a luxuriant moustache to match, and carried inside the school. I told him I'd broken my leg, but he didn't believe me.

'I have. I know I have.'

'You've probably just sprained your ankle.' He smiled an indulgent smile. 'It might feel like a break, but it will only be a sprain.'

It wasn't. It was a break, and I came back to school a few weeks later with my leg in plaster – the headmistress having thoughtfully sent me work to do at home so that I wouldn't fall behind.

I rather enjoyed the fuss of it all. Everybody signed my plaster cast, from the headmistress to the older girls in the second form that I rather took a fancy to.

Then came the day when I had to have the plaster cut off. We journeyed by ambulance to the hospital in Otley, where I was sized up by a particularly beefy nurse who reached inside a cupboard and pulled out what looked like a large pair of secateurs. With her tongue sticking out of the side of her mouth, the better to concentrate, she set to work snipping right down the side of the plaster. I kept deadly quiet, convinced that if she was distracted only for a second, the clippers would slip and I could say goodbye to my leg.

After the final snip, the plaster came away, to reveal a shrunken, withered leg that was covered in wisps of cotton wool. I tried to stand on it and fell over. The nurse laughed. 'It won't be ready for that yet, but we'll give you a pair of crutches and you can use them until it's strong enough.'

The crutches were too big and they hurt my arms. I felt particularly sorry for myself.

The ambulance took us home again, and I sat in a chair by the fire feeling like a cross between Colin in *The Secret Garden* and Clara in *Heidi* while my mother went out for the afternoon. She was quieter than usual and I couldn't work out why.

Cookie, our next-door neighbour, came in to look after me, and early in the evening my mother returned, weeping. I watched as she sat down by the fire holding her head in her hands, and seeing her so upset, I burst into tears.

That afternoon, as I had been having my plaster cut off, Grandma Hardisty had died in hospital. The doctor said it was a peaceful end. She was sixty-eight.

My mother was distraught. When my father came home that evening, they disappeared into the kitchen together as they always did on his return from work so they could chew over the events of the day. Then the door would be opened again and family life would resume. The door stayed closed longer than usual on this particular evening, and when eventually it opened again, I could see that they were both red-eyed.

Just a few days later I was taken to see Grandad Hardisty in hospital. He had been admitted while my grandma had also been there, but they had not told her. Neither had they told him that she had died.

He was being treated for an ulcer. I didn't know what that meant. I just knew he didn't look right, lying back on the pillow with a brown rubber tube going up his nose.

We stayed for an hour, my mother sitting by his bed and rubbing the back of his hand. Grandad didn't say much. He was very pale.

A few days later he died. At seventy-two, he was four years older than Grandma, but it was always she who wore the trousers.

Once over her initial grief, my mother quickly came to terms with the simultaneous loss of both her parents, difficult as it must have been. She likely as not took the same attitude with herself when it came to health – emotional or physical – as she did with her children.

She sat me on her knee one afternoon and tried to explain why, just a few weeks before, I had had three grandparents and now only one of them – Grandma Titchmarsh – was left.

'It is,' she said, 'the nicest thing, really, if you think about it.'

'But why? Why can it be nice that Grandma and Grandad have gone?'

'Because Grandad and Grandma loved one another very much. They'd always done things together. All their lives.'

'So?'

'Now they are together again.'

'But why is that good?' I simply could not see the logic.

'Well, you see, Grandad was the man, and men are always in charge of the house.'

'Yes?'

'But Grandma could always get him to do what she wanted.' Some parallel with her own relationship must have struck her here, as she quickly qualified the remark: 'But only because he would always look after her and do kind things to make sure she was happy.'

'So she wanted him to die?'

'Not really.'

'What, then?'

'Well, she'd probably have been lonely without him. And he wouldn't have been able to cope without her, would he? We know that.' Her eyes had a faraway look now. 'So, you see, I think she just whispered in his ear, when she'd gone.'

'Whispered what?'

'"Come on, Herbert." And what did your grandad do whenever your grandma said, "Come on, Herbert"?'

I did not need to think about my reply.

'He just went.'

Mum nodded and her eyes filled with tears. 'That's right,' she said. 'He just went.'

The relief must have been enormous when Mum and Dad found their own house. Number 34 Nelson Road was nothing grand. A bit bigger than 9 Dean Street, but with exactly the same number of rooms. It cost £800, and the mortgage was still being paid fourteen years later when we upped sticks as a family for the last time.

We moved into Nelson Road in 1950 and my dad set to work to put the house to rights. He was always good with his hands and so he turned the cellar into a workshop and began to do what all couples did in the 1950s and that was to make a Victorian house into something more 'contemporary'.

The brass doorknobs were banished and the door mouldings removed. Each door was made 'flush' with hardboard and a smart plastic handle fixed to it at an angle of forty-five degrees. Ball catches were fitted everywhere. The doors were painted dove grey, which made a change from the dark-brown woodgrain stain that was used in both my grannies' houses.

Me Dad

'You wait till your dad gets home.' As a statement it doesn't rank high in the intimidation stakes, but to lots of northern kids, 'Dad' represented the ultimate threat. If mine did, it was on a reluctant basis. He was never a violent man. Quite the reverse. He would do almost anything for a quiet life, but when rattled by my bad behaviour, he could run up the stairs three at a time with the whalebone hairbrush, even though he was only five feet eight.

I have the feeling that Dad considered himself the odd one out in his family. His father had died at the age of fifty-seven, when Dad was twenty, leaving a determined and beady-eyed widow, a daughter who was resigned to a life of disappointment and two sons – James and Alan.

Uncle Jim was nine years older than Dad, which would account, in part, for their lack of closeness as brothers. The other reason for their distancing could be put down to the fact that temperamentally they had little in common. Uncle Jim was lively and outgoing, a man who could spin out the simplest of stories to extravagant length. He was a dreadful joke-teller at our rare family parties and had a laugh that never quite made it into a guffaw. 'Tzzz, tzzz, tzzz,' it would go, and I could see my father bristling with irritation.

You could never call Dad irascible. Irritated, yes. And uncomfortable when his family embarrassed him. He positively bridled when Uncle Jim referred to him as 'our kid'. As a result he never sought out the company of his brother, or of his sickly sister; it was enough to turn up for the annual Boxing Day ordeal over the baize-covered table. At the end of the day we would leave with Dad under a cloud, ground down by the inconsequentialities of stilted conversation, and at the same time relieved that it was all over and done for another year. As far as his family was concerned, parties were not his strong point.

At home, he could be quiet and withdrawn, but not always in an unhappy way. My mother was a demanding woman to live with. She liked my dad at home with her, not out with the lads, as he was a couple of nights a week. When he came home from work on Christmas Eve afternoon having had a drink too many at lunchtime, he would be greeted with a tight-lipped silence. But he knew it would blow over if he kept his head down. She liked attention and most of the time Dad was happy to give it to her, but he could also retreat into his 'Yes, dear' mode, behind the pages of the *Daily Express*, which he could eke out for hours. My dad was the only person I knew who would read in detail the small ads in a national newspaper. For as long as it was held up in front of his face, he would be assured of peace and quiet.

I wouldn't want to make him sound humourless. He wasn't. Silly things would amuse him. He'd come downstairs from having a bath, beaming with delight and say, 'No links!' meaning that he'd filled the bath right up to the brim so that not a single link on the plug chain had been visible. He was not a man for aftershave, as a rule – reserving his Old Spice for special occasions – but he did come down from the bathroom one evening with the same beaming grin, saying, 'I've got everything on.' The tang of Old Spice was overlaid with that of Johnson's Baby Powder, which he clearly regarded as the height of sophistication.

He had phrases that he liked to use; 'It's immaterial to me' being one of them. 'I don't mind' would have done just as well, but he liked the word 'immaterial'. Mum said he got it from *Perry Mason*.

Deep down he was probably disappointed that he hadn't made more of his life. Even when he was called up during the war, he was not allowed to join the navy – the service he would have preferred – because he had flat feet. Instead, he joined the Royal Electrical and Mechanical Engineers (REME) and went out to India to repair tyres for Jeeps and lorries. He left school with no qualifications and became apprenticed to a plumber – three-quarter-inch nipples and ballcocks were his stock in trade for the rest of his life. He thought they might have made use of his skills when he was called up, and said he didn't remember mentioning tyres anywhere on the form.

Plumbing was not something he was passionate about. It was just what he did, where he found himself. He was never particularly ambitious, though there was a moment, towards the end of the 1950s, when he and Mum thought of emigrating to Canada, but it came to nothing. Dad would like as not have brought his usual caution to bear and thought the better of it.

Where he came into his own was around the house. He had an 'eye for a job', and while not exactly in the Colefax and Fowler class, his sense of proportion when it came to domestic construction was finely developed. Be it a breakfast bar or bookshelves, a new set of cupboards or a toy zoo, Dad could produce soundly made masterpieces from a few lengths of deal and some hardboard. What he could achieve with twenty feet of two-by-one and some quarter-inch ply was astonishing.

'Couldn't we make it more modern?' Mum asked, eyeing the front room up and down, glowering at the floor-to-ceiling cupboard in the corner and the blackened range that dominated her life. 'We could go contemporary.'

'If that's what you want.' My dad never expressed an audible opinion about interior design; Mum was the driving force, Dad the craftsman.

The range, with its glossy black doors and shiny steel hinges, was ripped out to reveal a yawning black hole, and replaced with a tiny cream-tiled fireplace whose colour was something between biscuit and beige.

Dad's vade mecum would be *Do-It-Yourself* magazine. Here were black-and-white pictures of a man in a collar and tie, smoking a pipe and sawing up a length of wood. There were complicated diagrams of kitchen units that seemed to have exploded, and handy hints on how to make your cylinder cupboard blend into the background on your landing. Mind you, Dad never had much time for Barry Bucknell, the handyman on the BBC, who had his panel pins already knocked in. 'He's made it all before,' muttered Dad, as though the broadcaster was cheating. Dad's preferred viewing was *Whirlybirds*, about two American helicopter pilots, Chuck and P.T. I think he'd have liked to have flown a helicopter, but in reality his life was much more grounded. He had his dreams, but stuck to what he was good at, and one by one the banes of Mum's 1950s' life would be replaced with modern counterparts.

Having been briefed by Mum as to her requirements, he would riffle through *Do-It-Yourself* every month for inspiration on how her dreams could be realised, and in the main they were. The kitchen cabinet with the drop-down front that gave out a high-pitched squeak as it was lowered into place on its metal rods was ousted in favour of the breakfast bar and buffets.

Fitted wardrobes replaced the fumed-oak monument in Mum and Dad's bedroom, and when my sister arrived and I moved up into the attic, fitted bookshelves and a desk were built against the wall and covered in dark-grey marble-effect Fablon. It was a feature I was ridiculously proud of – not just because it was better than the piddling little wooden desk that Mickey Hudson had in his bed-room, but because my dad had made it with his own bare hands.

None of the other dads in the street seemed to do anything like that. They could hang a bit of wallpaper and put a new plug on an electric fire, but those were jobs that anyone could do. They shied away from anything structural. But my dad could do everything.

He fitted a solid-fuel boiler in the kitchen, to take over the role of the big black range, and plumbed radiators into the bedrooms. They weren't new; he'd pulled them out of some house up the Grove where they were being replaced with newer models, but he thought they'd be 'just the job' for us, so he brought them home and plumbed them in.

I'd crouch down beside him while he worked away in his blue bib-and-brace overalls, smelling of putty and flux and that funny soft rope he used to seal the joints.

The blowlamp would roar as he melted the solder on the copper piping, and eventually would come the magic moment when he'd turn on the water supply.

'Put your hand on it, Algy, and tell me when it gets hot.'

I would lay my hand on the top of the fat, creamy-coloured radiator and wait.

'It's there, Dad!'

'Is it hot, or just warm?'

I felt again. 'It's warm at the top, but it's hot lower down.'

'Hang on.' He'd wearily climb back up the stairs and pull a small brass key out of his pocket, slotting it over the tiny nut at the top right-hand corner of the radiator. The air would come out with a hiss as he turned it, and eventually there would be the sound of bubbling and spitting, and a little squirt of blackened water would dribble into the plastic beaker he held underneath it, so as not to make a mess on Mum's rug.

Every night at bedtime this process was repeated by Mum. It became a sort of ritual. I assumed that's what you had to do with any form of central heating. It seemed a small price to pay for the warmth it provided. My dad never did let me into the intricacies of airlocks in plumbing, but then in our tall, narrow Victorian house they were probably a mystery to him, too.

On Friday nights Mum and Dad would go out together, but on Tuesdays Dad went out alone. To the fire station to do maintenance. He was a part-time fireman, Ilkley being too small to warrant a full-time crew. Instead, the engine was manned by local tradesmen and council workers, who would drop everything when the 'fire buzzer' wailed over the town, or during the night when the electric bell at the bottom of the stairs rang.

Dad would be up and out of bed within seconds, pulling on his trousers and shirt and fastening his shoes while muttering under his breath before running out of the door to the fire station in Golden Butts Road, two streets away.

If the buzzer went during the day, you'd see the firemen drop what they were doing and hare along the streets of the town. The engine took a limited crew of eight men, and only those who were quick enough or close enough to get there first would be paid the full whack. The others would be on standby.

In the early days the engine was open and the firemen stood on long steps that ran down the side of the scarlet-and-chrome 'appliance', as Dad called it. A huge ladder sloped upwards from the back of the engine to the front, terminating in two enormous cartwheels. If we were home from school, we'd run down the road to see if the engine came our way, waving at Dad in his tall fireman's hat as he clung on with one hand and fastened the chrome buttons of his thick navy-blue tunic with the other. The man seated next to the driver rang the big silver bell, and those with a free hand waved back as the gleaming machine hurtled down the road, the clanging bell eventually receding into the distance.

While fairly fleet of foot himself, Dad was not as driven as some of the retained firemen. He was especially scathing of Philip Dobson – smaller even than Dad – who wore black pumps all the time when he was at home, the better to increase the speed of his sprint. He lived only a street away from the fire station, so he had a head start when it came to making the engine. I felt sorry for his wife, a rather sad-looking lady called Maureen. If Philip happened to be drinking a cup of coffee, or having his tea on his lap in front of the fire, at the sound of the bell or the buzzer, up would go the plate or the cup – tossed in the air in the interest of speed – and his wife would be left to clean up the mess while he shot off like a greyhound from a trap.

'Daft,' was Dad's only remark.

We never stopped for a moment to consider the implications of Dad being a fireman. Certainly Mum never spoke about it. But she must have worried. Not about the chimney fires, or when he had to rescue cats from up trees. But Ilkley is near the mill towns of Keighley and Silsden, and when there was a mill fire, our men would be called in as reinforcements.

Mill fires invariably happened at night, and we'd all be woken by the bell in the early hours of the morning. I'd stir, and see the narrow shaft of light below my bedroom door that showed Dad was up and about to go. I'd turn over and go back to sleep without a thought for his safety. He never seemed to worry about it, so why should I? Then one Sunday morning he said it was time I saw what he did.

There had been a call-out during the previous Friday night, and I was aware that by Saturday morning Dad was still not back. Mum said that it was a mill fire in Keighley, and that they were still trying to put it out. At four in the afternoon, Dad returned, worn out and blackened with soot.

For the first time there was something in his eyes that I did not recognise, apart from the bone-weariness that seemed to have overtaken his body. I suppose, on reflection, that it was fear. Mum went up and hugged him, in spite of the fact that his face and hands were filthy. I thought it was odd; Mum always made Dad wash his hands before he gave her 'a love' when he came home from work. Today she didn't bother, just buried her head in his neck and held him tight. I went out of the back kitchen and into the garden; at moments like this I knew to leave them alone, and anyway, it was embarrassing.

On the Sunday morning he bundled us into the van and drove up through Steeton and Silsden to the outskirts of Keighley. There, at the side of the road, was a hole, an enormous hole, where two days previously a woollen mill had stood. Now there was hardly anything left of it. The outer stone walls, once robust and sturdy, had caved inwards into a gigantic pit. At the bottom of the pit was a confused tangle of machinery and masonry. But the thing that made the greatest impression were the gigantic steel girders that had once held the floors of the mill. They must have been three feet wide, but they were twisted and tangled and knotted like spaghetti on top of the smouldering wreckage. So great was the heat that they had buckled and melted, allowing the entire building to fall in on itself.

I turned to look at Dad, who was gazing silently at the wreckage. The dampness of steam and the rank odour of smouldering, saturated wool lay heavily on the air.

'Where were you?' I asked.

Dad pointed to the other side of the building. 'Over there,' he said. 'On top of a ladder. I just kept pointing my hose at the flames.'

'Was it hot?'

'Yes, very.'

'How long did they take to go out?'

'Twelve hours.'

He didn't seem to want to talk any more, so I stopped asking questions. After that, whenever the fire buzzer went off or the bell rang at the bottom of our stairs, I felt uneasy until my dad was safely back in the house and life was returned to normal.

I never thought of him as a hero. It was just what he did. But Mum was unusually quiet whenever he was out at a fire. She knew there was an ever-present danger and a real risk of loss of life. It had happened to other firemen in nearby stations; if I'd taken the trouble to interpret her mood, I might have been more worried than I was.

That my mother loved my father deeply I never doubted. Apart from her flirting with other men – which didn't amount to more than a lowering of the eyelids and a coy note in her voice – she never had eyes for anyone else. I never heard them swapping terms of endearment, or saw them being overly demonstrative in public apart from holding hands when we went out for a walk, but every evening when Dad came home from work and my sister and I were playing in the front room, the door between the front room and the kitchen would be closed and we would hear the muffled sound of Mum and Dad telling each other the gossip of the day, interspersed with the occasional kiss. Each morning, when she'd made his 'packing' – sandwiches and a boiled egg wrapped in waxed paper, a Penguin biscuit and a flask of tea neatly fitted into the khaki canvas bag that he slung over his shoulder – they'd hug and have the regulation three kisses before he left: two short ones and a long one on the lips. They never minded us seeing that.

She hated him being ill. He caught pneumonia just after my sister was born and was chivvied by my mother into being well again. Later on in life he had a heart scare and the nurses in the hospital used to dread the effect that my mother's visit would have on his blood pressure. She didn't mean to be unkind; she just needed him to be at home with her. That she exasperated him there is no doubt. She was not always reasonable in her demands. But they fitted together with the comfortableness of two people who knew each other's strengths and weaknesses, and who also knew, from the day they married in 1947, that they would be together for the rest of their lives. It was taken for granted.

Every now and then he'd look at her and wink and say, 'All right, Beff?' and she'd nod and smile at him with a sparkle in her eyes.

They'd go on Wallace Arnold coach tours later in life, when my sister and I had flown the nest. They liked the Forest of Dean best, and once were daring enough to go to Austria. Arthritic by now, Mum had a little metal shield with 'Steinach' nailed on to her walking stick as a memento.

When Dad died of a heart attack at the age of sixty-two in 1986, her world fell apart, and until her own death in 2002, at the age of seventy-eight, she had no interest in any other man. But then, as she told the vicar at Dad's funeral, 'He was the best thing that ever happened to me.' It was as simple as that.

A lack of inches did little for my confidence. I was shorter than the other boys right from the start, and I struggled for years to believe that I was here for any other reason than to make up the numbers – a belief reinforced by the fact that along with the fat boy I was always the last one to be picked in the line-up for the football team. My lack of confidence didn't manifest itself in chippiness; instead, it translated into chirpiness, which to those around me must have been even more irritating. It was nothing more than an attempt to prove that I was just one of them, even if I didn't really feel that I was. My lasting memories of junior school and secondary school are of being told to shut up. My crime, if anything, was that of being too enthusiastic.

Even my earliest school experiences came as a bit of a shock. Mum clearly loved me; I knew that, even though 'I love you' was not a phrase that was ever used in our house. We weren't that soft. But if she did love me, why didn't she want to be with me all day? It was a puzzle.

Skewell

B efore I started school, I was packed off three or four days a
week to the state-run nursery down by the allotments. It was a
pre-war prefab, staffed by a few kindly ladies who let us paint a lot
and insisted that we rest on canvas stretchers after lunch, when all we
really wanted to do was run around.

There was only one compensation as far as I was concerned: after
the early-afternoon doze on the stretcher, and a brief breath of fresh
air wearing sun hats to stop us from getting freckles, they combed
my hair and dipped the comb in water to give my fringe a quiff. If
they forgot, I used to remind them. My mum always admired it
when she came to take me home, but she never had the knack of
recreating that particular style, however hard she tried. At home, I
lived with the floppy fringe.

Six months later things were completely different. There were no
early-afternoon dozes and quiffs at Ilkley New County Infants,
down Leeds Road. This was a proper school, newly built from local
sandstone and run by the severe headmistress Miss Howker.

Mrs Osman took the first class – she seemed as old as God with her
long, white hair, and wore a floral-print overall in which she floated
about the classroom. Her frame was as slight as a wraith, and her
voice was reedy – frequently breaking into another octave when she
tried to raise the volume, which she did, it seemed, every couple of
minutes.

'I'm going to draw something on the blackboard now and you're
going to tell me what it is,' she would croak.

Hands would shoot up all over the classroom.

'It's a beetle, miss.'

75

'No, miss, it's a spider.'

Mrs Osman would look crestfallen.

'No. It's a sheep.'

We tried our best not to look disbelieving. She was a nice lady, though no Elisabeth Frink, and we didn't want to disappoint her.

'And what do sheep say?'

'Bugger all,' muttered Buster Stirk.

'No, Buster. They say, "Baaa."'

And so it is that whenever I think of Mrs Osman and her creaky, croaky voice, I think of sheep bleating.

In charge of the second year was the young and athletic Miss Outersides with well-developed calves and a mane of dark-brown hair – a sort of Eileen Fowler for infants. Whatever the weather, Miss Outersides wore a brown tweed skirt and white pumps, equipping her all the better to run after some recalcitrant child bent on going home early. You'd frequently see her bounding figure flashing past the classroom window. She ran silently, thanks to the pumps, and was adept at capturing her escaping charge just before he made the painted iron gates that opened on to the outside world. The ear would usually be the first point of contact, but Miss Outersides had a knack of never inflicting pain – just remorse.

Where Mrs Osman creaked and croaked, Miss Outersides boomed. I suppose she was just out of college, and her enthusiasm, coupled with her athletic bearing, drove her through the school like a brisk breeze. When she read us a story, late in the afternoon, her brisk delivery meant that it wasn't so much a fairy tale, more an instruction manual.

The third class was taken by dark-haired Mrs Smith, who had a snooty daughter called Roberta who went to a posh school somewhere else. She came in every now and again at the end of the day, and could turn her head so fast that her long plaits could sting your eyes. She was very good at sweeping off in a huff. I don't know why. Maybe she just resented being there. Mrs Smith's husband had a bubble car, and sometimes he'd come and collect the two of them at the end of the afternoon. This was when Roberta got her comeuppance. It's difficult to be indignant when you're sitting in the back of a bubble car.

Miss Howker herself took charge of the seniors, who would be all of seven years old. She was a no-nonsense matriarch who gave the appearance of having a leg at each corner, and while not exactly having a ready temper, her look alone could stop a six-year-old hooligan in his tracks. Not for her the floral-print overall or the speedy white pumps. Miss Howker wore a pleated skirt, a navy-blue jumper and pearls. Without fail. She had glasses that she would look over to silence an unwanted conversation, and an invitation to see her in her office would cause the colour to drain from the face of the toughest young lad. It was said that she had a stick.

Number 9 Dean Street abutted on to the school playing field, but I don't remember seeing much of Grandma and Auntie Alice, even on washing day; instead, I remember sports days and endless games of the farmer's in his den with Mrs Tillotson, the portly dinner lady. She looked like a farmer's wife herself, and we all loved her. She minded our manners while we ate and, if we were reluctant, spooned the last few mouthfuls of some sickly dessert into our unwilling mouths. She'd make up for this immediately afterwards by taking us out into the playground. Sometimes, if one or two of us were feeling a bit off colour, she'd let us hold her hand. One sports day my mum had turned up late, holding a hanky over her mouth. She'd been to the dentist to have a tooth out and so couldn't join in the parents' race. She couldn't even speak. She just shook her head and then, after all the races, she went home before I did. I was disappointed. I knew that if she'd joined in, she'd have won. She was a good runner.

Mrs Tillotson spotted my sadness and came over to the chain-link fencing where I stood, watching my mum, hanky clutched to face, walking home without me. Mrs Tillotson took my hand and led me back across the thick green grass towards the tarmac playground where the other kids were playing happily.

'Never mind. Here . . . I've got something for you.' She dipped her hand into her pocket and brought out a single lead soldier. It was nothing special. A bit battered. Just a soldier in khaki standing to attention, his hat so worn that the shiny grey lead was showing through.

'Would you like it?' she asked.

I nodded and murmured, 'Yes, please.'

'Go on, then. You keep it.' She took my hand again and walked me towards the school. 'It reminds me of my son. He's in the army. Doing national service. Out in Malaya.'

'Oh.' I didn't know what national service was, except that it sounded important. Mrs Tillotson went quiet for a bit, and then she said, 'Let's play the farmer's in his den.'

Soon we had all linked hands and begun to walk round in a circle, as Mrs Tillotson in her quavering soprano began the chant: 'The farmer's in his den, the farmer's in his den, ee-eye-enjy-o, the farmer's in his den,' we sang as we walked around in a circle, vying to be the ones who held Mrs Tillotson's hand, rather than those who were spirited into the centre of the circle to play the named parts of farmer, wife, dog and bone. Woe betide you if you got to be the bone given to the farmer's dog. The last verse was 'We all pat the bone', and the game usually ended with 'the bone' suffering mild concussion. Other than that, life at infant school was not especially risky, except for encounters with Kitty Oldacre and rhubarb and custard.

Kitty was small and blonde with dark eyebrows and a winning smile. She seemed to wear party frocks every day and I looked at her in wonder and amazement, until the day she decided to clean out her left nostril with the pompom on her lemon-yellow cardigan.

'Kitty Oldacre, stop that,' warned Mrs Smith. 'You do not use your pompom to remove nose dirt.'

I never knew why she didn't just say 'snot', but I never looked at Kitty Oldacre in the same way after that. And I didn't look at rhubarb and custard either. Not after Mrs Tillotson stood over me while I finished it off. It tasted sour.

'I'm going to be sick,' I said.

'No you're not. It's just nerves. Now get those last few mouthfuls down and then we'll go out and play, there's a good boy.'

By this time I was the only child left in the cavernous school hall, and the hands on the clock with the coloured numbers high up on the wall were showing playtime ticking away.

I did my best with that rhubarb, and I did, in the end, get it all down. But in spite of Mrs Tillotson's encouragement, and in spite of the fact that I wanted to please her, it was all to no avail. Within seconds the rhubarb and custard was back up again and Mrs Tillotson went off in search of a bucket and mop.

I can eat rhubarb and custard quite happily now. But the smell of school disinfectant can still make me break out into a cold sweat.

Junior school, up Leeds Road, was even more trying, not least because of the robust lady who presided over the first form. Mrs Richardson could have taught Mussolini a thing or two about discipline and organisation. While I am sure that at home she was a kind and loving mother with a fondness for dogs and needlepoint, at school she could, under the right circumstances, become a spitting volcano of contumely.

Dahn Leeds Road

Almost as wide as she was high, Mrs Richardson had a mop of curly hair that quivered when she was angry. Under these circumstances, it was wise not to get too close, for two reasons. The first was her saliva, which could be projected a good six feet, and the second was her right index finger and thumb, which, when applied to the hairs at the back of your neck and twisted, could bring tears to the eyes of the toughest pupil.

You could see these raging furies begin to build. First she would blink a lot, then she would raise her voice, and when the words 'You big blockheads!' tumbled out of her mouth, you knew that the twisted hair could not be far away.

She'd be sacked now. But none of us would have wished that on her. We just wished she wouldn't shout quite so loud when we were close by. And to be fair, it was Mrs Richardson who showed me how to get roots to grow on pussy willow (by doing nothing more than standing the stems in a jar of water), and to get broad-bean seeds to germinate on damp blotting paper up the sides of a large pickled-onion jar.

The words 'plumule' and 'radicle' I learned at the tender age of eight.

'What is the seed-coat for?' asked Mrs Richardson.

'To keep the seed warm, miss?' offered Peter Earle.

'Stupid boy,' she muttered under her breath. Then she tapped on her desk to emphasise the words: 'What . . .' tap '. . . is the seed-coat . . .' tap '. . . for?'

He should have noticed the warning signs. The nostrils were flaring already. But Peter Earle was always a risk-taker.

83

'Miss, it's because you keep pouring all that cold water on it. It's reet nithered.'

'You big blockhead . . .' She was marching towards him already. Those sitting on either side of the aisle ducked to avoid the spit. Peter Earle tried to back away, but he had made a tactical error. His chair was up against the wall. Being good at asserting himself, he had made sure of that when we first came into the classroom back in September. He knew winter was coming and spotted the thick iron central-heating pipes that emerged from the wall at that point. If he got a desk by them, he'd never be cold – the caretaker was short on generosity when it came to coke. But now he had discovered the disadvantages of his placement. He put one foot up on the pipes with the intention of teetering along them and out of reach, but he failed in his attempt and one leg slid behind the pipes, effectively anchoring him to the spot.

In the blinking of one of her beady eyes, Mrs Richardson had brought the pincer movement to bear on the back of his neck and Peter's ginger hair was already being twisted into an agonising plait.

'Aw, no, miss . . . No!'

'Mechanical damage! The seed-coat is there to prevent mechanical damage.'

Peter screwed up his eyes. 'Miss . . . yer damaging *me*!' he wailed.

'And to absorb water to allow germination.' She paused to let the words sink in. 'What is the seed-coat for?'

Rapidly her victim blurted out the words, 'To prevent mechanical damage, miss . . .'

'And . . . ?'

'To ab . . . to ab . . .'

'TO ABSORB WATER AND ALLOW . . . ?'

'Extermination, miss.'

It was the final straw. Mrs Richardson released her grip and for a moment Peter Earle thought he had escaped. A look of relief flashed across his face. But not for long. The flat of the teacher's hand caught him smartly on the back of the head, flicking it forward and propelling the startled boy clear of the radiator. For a brief moment he seemed airborne, and then he landed with a thud, spread-eagled across his desk like a young bird attempting its first flight.

'Aw . . . that's not fair, miss! I couldn't hear 'cos you were twistin'
me 'air.'

'Silly little boy. Pay attention in future.'

Peter Earle looked suitably humiliated and sat down meekly
behind his desk. Mrs Richardson's fury subsided as swiftly as it
had erupted and now she was beaming at us and asking, 'And what is
the first seed-leaf called?'

I knew. But I didn't want to risk it.

Peter Earle was the daredevil of junior school. Ginger and freckled,
he was born reckless and was always the first to do anything that
could be described as risky. He had a sidekick, a burly lad with dark
hair and glasses called Ian Gledhill. Ian never seemed to actually do
anything, or even speak, but he was always there. He was a sort of
conjuror's assistant – his presence made whatever stunt was being
perpetrated seem more official. He would gaze at Peter Earle in
silent and admiring wonder, but then his mentor did have certain
capabilities lacking in the rest of us.

Peter Earle was far and away the loudest belcher in the school.
And he could do it to order. He found enormous pleasure in
letting fly a particularly loud one – the sort that if well aimed
would echo off the stone wall of the boys' toilets – when any
female teacher went by, first taking great care to make sure that he
was masked by other bodies, any one of which could, strategically,
have been responsible for the sound. But they knew it was him
and, in spite of his protestations, would haul him out for a clip
round the ear. He stopped after a while, seeing little point in not
getting away with it, and instead perfected the SBD – the fart that
was silent but deadly.

His diet was the subject of much conjecture, and his timing was
unerringly theatrical. He could release his particular brand of poison
gas seemingly at will in the most sensitive part of the lesson – just
when the story was being told at the end of the day and we were
about to reach the bit where Umslopogaas rescued Alan Quatermain. Mr Swann, the teacher, would adopt an attitude in keeping
with his name and remain serene, pretending that nothing had

happened. He would plod along determinedly with the story, although the observant may have noticed a very slight watering of the eyes.

The pupils were less reserved. They daren't make a noise while the story unfolded, but one by one they would clamp their fingers and thumbs to their noses until they looked like a phalanx of swimmers about to jump into deep water. A daring few would fan the air with their hands, and Peter Earle would smile serenely, pretending that he didn't know what was the matter, before clamping his own finger and thumb to his nose when Mr Swann looked up from Allan Quatermain's adventures, lest it should be obvious that he was the perpetrator.

His other tricks varied with the seasons. Autumn was his favourite. There was a row of chestnut trees at the back of the church. He joined the choir for the first crack at getting the conkers down with a stick, as much as for the money you got for singing at weddings. His stick was always bigger and heavier than anybody else's, and when he lobbed it high into the branches, you kept out of the way if you had any sense.

Why he bothered to search for the largest of the conkers was beyond me, because when he'd found them, and threaded them on to the end of a piece of string, he threaded a steel nut on to the other. Having lulled you into a false state of security, with your own conker soaked in vinegar and cooked in the oven to make it harder, he would wait until a few hits had been accomplished and then, with deft sleight of hand, turn round the piece of string and assail yours with the lump of steel.

We knew that he cheated. Every time. But for some reason it was accepted as being his normal standard of behaviour, and when you got used to being duped yet again, it somehow added a bit of spice to school life.

Bonfire Night was his other high spot. Well, not so much the night as the season that brought fireworks into the shops. Not for him the gentle delights of golden rain and roman candle, Catherine wheel and mine of serpents. No. He was interested only in bangers – the louder the better.

86

The penny bangers were OK, but they went off with a 'phutt' rather than a bang.

'Yer don't want them,' he boasted. 'Yer want these big buggers.'

He pulled his hand out of his pocket to reveal a fistful of threepenny cannons. The threepenny cannons had sides of thick cardboard and they made a proper bang. The sort that could frighten a girl out of her skin. But he tired of lobbing them at girls after a while, and looked for a modus operandi that would involve more risk.

His bike – unlike those of the rest of us, which had ordinary handlebars or, at best, straight ones – had cow-horn handlebars and no mudguards. Our mums wouldn't let us go for either of these options. If you had no mudguards, your school uniform got splashed with mud from the back wheel, and cow-horn handlebars were unsafe. (Quite how, I never had the nerve to enquire.)

But Peter had somehow got away with both. Maybe his mother had bigger things to worry about. With Ian Gledhill looking on and holding the box of matches, Peter took a roll of Sellotape and strapped two of the threepenny cannons to each of the back forks of his bike.

On a muddy knoll on the edge of the moor, he'd brief us on what he was about to attempt. Ian would light the fuses on the fireworks, and Peter would then pedal off down the hill. At a strategic point on the track – just where there was a deep and muddy puddle – the bangers would go off.

We listened in silence, and watched intently as Peter mounted the bike, grasped the handlebars and nodded to his assistant, who struck a match and quickly lit the bangers on either side of the bike before retiring.

With no backward glance, Peter pushed off from the top of the hill and hurtled downwards towards the muddy swamp at the bottom. As his front wheel ploughed into the mud, so the back one was lifted three feet into the air by the explosion of the four threepenny cannons. The whole bike twisted, hung in the air for the briefest of moments, and then plunged downwards into the quagmire below.

A deft twist of his body was all it took for Peter to remain upright and to avoid following his bike into the swamp. All that could be seen of it now was the end of one of the handlebars. He hauled it out, and came back up the hill with the mud-covered machine and a beaming grin. 'Good, eh?' he asked.

We nodded and smiled admiringly. The spectacle had been well worth watching, and the skill with which he had dismounted the bike in mid-air had been quite breathtaking. But what we were more curious about was what his mother would say when he got home. By cleverly swivelling his bike in mid-air he'd avoided landing in the quagmire, but the lack of a back mudguard and the force of the four threepenny cannons had combined to produce an unfortunate effect. We didn't like to tell him, but as he pushed his machine back down Cowpasture Road with a beaming Ian Gledhill in tow, he looked for all the world as though he'd shit himself.

For a lad who liked 'playing out', Ilkley was a pretty good place to grow up, all things considered. It's a predominantly Victorian town, built of local sandstone (long since blackened by soot) to house the wool merchants of Leeds and Bradford when there were enough of them to make it worthwhile. It was famous for its waters, too, back in the days when the maxim 'If it tastes bad, it must be good for you' carried some clout, and there were Gothic-towered 'hydropathic establishments' on the edge of the moor where posh people would pay to be treated badly. It was called a health cure.

The tatty red guidebook to the town that sat on our bookshelf listed eight different hydros. By the time I came along, they had all been converted into hotels or flats or, in one case, the College of Housecraft, where I presumed that nice girls learned about cooking and knitting.

Craiglands Hotel, where my dad did the plumbing, had become Ilkley's poshest hotel by the 1950s, but a century earlier it was described in the guidebook as 'the largest hydro in Yorkshire', and in addition to its mission to cure, it boasted 'a constant round of varied entertainments every night throughout the year'.

When the residents had recovered from this nightly hilarity, they could look forward to the fact that 'Allopathic remedies are used wherever deemed advisable. Under the watchful superintendence of Dr Dobson, the resident medical superintendent, modern hydropathy is applied in every form that science, experience and observation can suggest. To modern hydropathy may be added mustard pads, massage, electricity, etc. Crises are avoided.' Which must have reassured potential inmates. It cost them between £1 18s 6d and £2 12s

6d per week to avail themselves of these irresistible amenities. Fifty years later my dad made sure they all still worked.

Its Gothic torture chambers apart, Ilkley is a picturesque town, especially from a distance. Snuggled down in the bottom of the dale, it looks as though it would rather you didn't notice it. If you climb on to the edge of Rombald's Moor and haul yourself up on to the big lumps of millstone grit that are known as the Cow and Calf, you'll see the town spread out below you, running from left to right along the silvery ribbon of the River Wharfe. Silvery when the sun shines on it, anyway. Dark brown when it doesn't. The colour of strong beer.

Down By the River

Of the three options that my mother would offer of a Sunday – moors, woods or river – the river was the one that would most frequently get my vote. The moors are rugged and majestic with far-reaching views, Middleton Woods dark and mysterious except when carpeted by bluebells in May, but the River Wharfe is a romantic watercourse at any time of year. It is moody, and changeable, a raging and destructive torrent in times of high rainfall, but in its calmer moments it has a friendliness that the other two cannot match. It starts its life springing like burst veins of milk from the slopes of Oughtershaw Side and Cam Rakes at the top of the dale and finally pours itself into the Yorkshire Ouse at Cawood near Selby, submerging its delicate character in its more muscular partner without a backward glance. That's the sort of prose that would have sent Miss Weatherall, my English teacher, reaching for her red Biro and penning, in her annoyingly neat hand, at the bottom of my essay 'Too much imagination, Titchmarsh; straight from *Chick's Own*,' whatever that was.

But the Wharfe is a river that induces flights of fancy and affection. John Ruskin wrote that 'If ever one was metamorphosed into a river, and could choose one's own size, it would be out of all doubt more prudent and delightful to be Wharfe than Rhône.' The difference is that the Wharfe gives rise to beer rather than wine where it runs over limestone at Tadcaster. There, over the years, the two Smiths – John and Samuel – and Mrs Tetley's lad, Joshua, have produced their 'clear beer' for the enjoyment of the locals and those wistful Yorkshiremen far from home who look upon the county of their birth as a kind of Shangri-La, and its beer as a tangible way of keeping at least a bit of their homeland quite literally flowing through their veins.

Oughtershaw and Cam Fell were just names in a guidebook when I was little. The farthest upstream we got was to the Strid at Bolton Abbey. It's a narrowing of the waters that boils in a turbulent current through the gap between two large boulders and where in the Middle Ages, as we had been told in hushed tones at school, the boy Egremond, son of Alice Romilly, had drowned, thanks to hanging on to the lead of his reluctant greyhound when out walking one morning. His mother never recovered from her grief and so we felt it only fair not to put our own mothers to the same trouble. We kept well away from the edge.

But further downstream, at Burnsall and Bolton Abbey, where the beer-brown waters – rich in minerals from their journey over a billion boulders – danced by more slowly, we were allowed to paddle and to skim an endless supply of smooth and shallow stones across the deeper water.

On the stretch of river at Ilkley between the Old Bridge, an elegant stone construction built in 1675, and the metal footbridge known as the swing bridge (even though it did not), I was allowed to go and play on my own. Happily. Allowed for a day to disappear with my imagination into another world.

But first I'd need the fishing net. It would be bought from Mr Marshall's sweet shop at the bottom of Brook Street on the first fine Sunday of the year. A clutch of nets – some blue, some pink – each attached to a five-foot bamboo pole, would be stuffed into an umbrella stand on the pavement, along with twittering birds that you could swirl round your head on a string. I'd pick out the net I wanted – always blue – and go in to hand over the shilling to Mr Marshall, who would be standing on a raised walkway behind his counter, towering over the steep slope of glass-lidded boxes of wafer biscuits and Wagon Wheels, giant jars of humbugs and chocolate eclairs, sherbet-filled flying saucers and penny chews. Mr Marshall would always be chewing something himself. Free samples probably. He had the best job in the world. It must have been. At the back of the shop, he sold electric trains. Sweets at the front and electric trains at the back – his wasn't a job; it was a dream.

Early on a summer's morning during the school holidays, I would fetch a jam jar from the cellar. Dad would have a piece of rough and hairy string in his plumber's tool bag. I'd make a handle out of it. Along with the bamboo pole with the fishing net, it would be all I needed for a day out. That and a jam sandwich and a bottle of pop.

But there were rules. I was allowed to go off on my own all day with a simple 'Be careful', but I was not allowed any old pop. Tizer was out. So, too, were cream soda and dandelion and burdock. They rotted your teeth, along with cherryade. I could have lemonade, or lemon and lime, or grapefruit. They were allowed. And so that's what I had. In a moment of rebellion, I might take a furtive swig of Mickey Hudson's dandelion and burdock, but I didn't like it much, not when it was warm and full of someone else's spit, and cream soda was sickly sweet; you could actually feel it eating into your teeth. There seemed little point in making a stand when I quite liked the limited range of fizzy drinks that had the maternal seal of approval, and especially if I didn't want to be like Angela Butterfield, who'd lost all her teeth from eating too many sweets by the age of twelve. Or so they said. She did have three left, but they weren't a pretty sight.

With the net over my shoulder and the jam jar dangling at my side, I could set off in my shorts, T-shirt and sandals – these would be last year's model with the fronts cut out to accommodate the toes that were now right up against the leather. I'd have a new pair every summer – watching the crêpe soles turning from their pristine creamy white to dark grey as the year wore on was one way of marking the passage of time. With the buckled straps now short enough to begin cutting into my bare ankles, I'd walk down past the gasworks, across the allotments between forests of rhubarb and blackberries and then along the riverbank to a suitable spot. Underneath the overhanging branches of a weeping willow that trailed its lower leaves into the water, I could take off the painful sandals and leave them with my picnic while I ventured out, tentatively, into the orange-coloured water, pulling up the legs of my shorts when I hit an unexpectedly deep spot, teetering when my sensitive feet hit a sharp stone, and all the while peering through the water for any fish that I could scoop up with the net.

Bullheads were the best bet – sluggish and easy to catch, with their wide heads and sulky expressions. Minnows lasted only an hour in the jar; as soon as the sun heated up the water, they lost the will to live and lay on the surface, their silver sides flashing accusingly in the sun. Catfish presented the greatest challenge. Only the most skilful fisherman could catch these sleek and whiskered beauties. They would nose upwards into the current, perfectly camouflaged in their infantry khaki against the mossy rocks. You would spot one, line up your net steadily behind it and then . . . pounce! Too late. The net would spring clear of the water empty except for a wisp of greeny-brown weed.

On a good day there would be a crayfish or two lurking beneath smooth boulders in the shallows, but crayfish took bravery to catch. You'd have to lift the rock and then quickly slide your hand underneath it, scrabbling around to see if one of them was hiding there. You might get a nip for your trouble, but it was worth it to see the grey-brown miniature lobster pirouetting at the bottom of your jam jar, desperate to find a way out.

I'd stand my jam jar and its inmate on the rich, green grassy bank at the water's edge, and lie down full length so that my eyes were level with those of the creature itself. Then I'd stare at it, telling myself that I should remember exactly what it looked like if I were to consider myself a proper naturalist like Peter Scott.

In an especially earnest mood, I'd have a notebook with me and jot down my findings – the colour of the fish, the number of fins, its approximate length and any other interesting features. It wasn't that I thought they would be of any assistance to the advancement of science, but such conscientiousness made me feel that hoiking the little blighters out of their home and risking their untimely deaths would not be totally wasted if it led to my increased knowledge.

On other days the observation of things less scientific would get the better of me. The glinting of the sun on the surface of the water and the millions of stars that flashed and disappeared in an instant.

The shape of a ripple. How could anybody possibly paint a picture of a river when it moved so quickly? And what was the biggest rock that could be hurled into the middle of the stream to make that deep-throated 'ker-plunk' with an after-splash that could reach six feet into the air?

The bottle of pop would be kept cool by immersion in the shallows, and no matter how hard I tried, it and the jam sandwiches would never last until dinnertime. Lunch was something that posh people had; we had breakfast, dinner and tea.

By half past twelve I'd be hungry, and would wend my way home to see if there was anything else to eat. The fish, after the first few disastrous attempts to keep them alive in a bigger jar in the backyard, were tipped gently back into the water, and the embryo naturalist returned home once more to satisfy his appetite for food rather than information.

Looking back on these lazy days, they seem impossibly Arcadian. As if I was enveloped in some Christopher Robin idyll. But then I was, though I never knew it at the time.

But all that changed when Cindy arrived. She had long, blonde hair, deep-blue eyes and as great a passion for the outdoors as I did. She was a corgi, cairn and border-terrier cross-breed, and she gave me any excuse I needed to escape the house and go out into the world.

Wharfedale is not as chocolate-box pretty in its lower reaches as Wensleydale or Swaledale, and not so famous either. But it's a good dale, a working dale, with light industry as well as agriculture doing its best to make up for the fortune that wool used to bring it. And there are houses. Lots of houses. People like living here and the 'heather spa', as the Victorians called it, has grown rapidly over the last fifty years.

There are still plenty of sheep here. This is not arable land. There are no prairies of corn, just pale-green undulating fields, hungry-looking, and bordered by drystone walls, often with a few strands of rusty wire stretched between old posts along the top edge, the better to stop the sheep from escaping. They speckle most of the fields that surround the town on all sides, and amble across the heather and bracken of the moors, getting in the way of cars when they scatter across the moorland roads. They have black faces, and shaggy grey coats, seemingly whatever the time of year. I suppose they must be sheared, but most of the time they seem overdressed and in need of a wash. Sometimes the odd one will make its way down Cowpasture Road and into the town, but only if it's nimble-footed.

'Get out of it, yer daft bugger!' was a frequently heard cry in childhood, before the cattle grids came.

For the first twenty years of my life, apart from one week's holiday a year in Blackpool, church-choir trips to Morecambe or the Lakes and a scout trip to London, I hardly ventured out of this valley. To travel far from the Wharfe made me nervous. I didn't feel especially unambitious, but to my way of thinking, if you lived

97

in a place that you liked, and which seemed to offer all that you needed, what was the point in looking further afield? News didn't happen where we were. It hardly even happened in Leeds. It happened in London, which might as well have been another country. My country was this one. The one I could see from the Cow and Calf. Big enough and varied enough for anyone. Well, big enough for me. For the time being.

The Lone Ranger and Cindy

T he Evanses had a basenji. Jane Evans used to boast about it. 'It's
the only dog in the world that doesn't bark.'

'It bloody bites, though,' muttered Dokey Gell, eyeing it up
warily. And it did. It was a snappy beggar. And the trouble was, you
couldn't hear it coming. You could tell which kids lived in our street
by their identity marks – the bites on their legs.

Philomena Forrest had Laddie, a perky little terrier the colour of
toffee, with sticky-up ears and a beard, and the rather shady family at
the top of the street had a brown-and-white springer spaniel that was
as scary as they were. It was completely bonkers. You could see it,
some mornings, chasing its tail in the middle of the road – round and
round in circles until the milkman eased it out of the path of his van
with a well-placed boot and it would run off yelping and cower
under a laurel bush for half an hour before coming out and starting
the game all over again.

Our first foray into dog ownership had not gone well. When I
was around two years old, my parents bought a blue-roan cocker
spaniel they called Brock. Within the year he fell victim to hard pad,
and after sitting up with him all night as he tried to climb the walls of
the front room, my mother took him to the vet and sat with him as
he was put to sleep. The experience so upset her that she vowed
never to have another dog. A cat would be better.

Unfortunately the kitten that was chosen turned out to be feral. It
climbed the curtains and tore at the furniture. When it started
tearing at my parents, my father decided enough was enough and
drowned it in a bucket of water. My mother said that he was never
the same again. Not with cats, anyway.

99

But eventually Mum must have overcome her grief as far as dogs were concerned, because one snowy Saturday morning in the winter of 1958, we walked to Ben Rhydding to go and choose a puppy.

The litter of corgi, cairn and border-terrier cross-breeds numbered around ten. All of them were smooth-haired, except for one: the one that refused to come and be looked at. She was a bitch, and far too intent on digging a burrow in the snow in the back garden to report for inspection and be sized up.

We looked at them all, and my mother and I (my sister being too small to be capable of making any decision, except when she needed to eat) tried to choose just one. It was difficult. They were all much the same except for the one with the long, blonde hair whose wagging tail was now the only thing visible for inspection. And there wasn't much of that. It had been docked, and looked like a hyperactive hamster.

Finally Mum decided that we would put them all in a line – or as much of a line as ten eight-week-old pups can be put in – and then call them. The one that came towards us first would be the one we took home.

The owner hauled the long-haired pup out of the snow and lined her up with the others as best she could.

'Go on, then, call them,' instructed my mother.

I crouched down, patted my knees and called. Not one of them moved. I called again. Nothing. The pups just stared at me, bewildered and confused. And then the long-haired digger in the snow cocked her head on one side, took one tentative step towards me and sealed her fate.

Why we called her something as twee as Cindy I don't know. It was short for Cinderella. Perhaps we'd been to the panto at Leeds Grand or Bradford Alhambra that year. But for the next fifteen years the family activities seemed to revolve around her.

She was a spirited dog, short in the leg, but big on courage. Not snappy, but with a decent bark on her to frighten away unwanted callers when my mother was at home alone, and, boy, could she run. She could swim, too. We'd take her down to the river, throw in a stick, and with one of us on the opposite bank we could get her to swim across and back again time after time. It was a miracle, bearing in mind the length of her legs – six inches at most.

Sometimes the current would take her perilously close to the Crum Wheel, a whirlpool in the bend of the river close to the woods, and about which fearful stories were told of men who'd lost their lives in its treacherous grip. In all my years there, the most serious loss was that of a small plastic boat that waltzed round in a circle for half an hour before eventually being washed downstream. Cindy did not become one of its casualties.

But our best times were up on the moors. There, in summer, the two of us would bowl downhill through the bracken seeing who could run the fastest. She would always win, and when I fell head over heels over some boulder and landed with a soft thump on the springy earth among the fern fronds, she'd retrace her steps to find me, licking my face to facilitate a full recovery.

She was never fed titbits from the table, but she was taught to sit and beg for a biscuit, which you could hold until you said, 'All right,' and she would take it neatly from your fingers without ever the feel of teeth on flesh.

Her musical attributes were discovered by accident. One Christmas I found a Hohner mouth organ in my stocking. I took it out of the box and began to play it – running up and down the scale, sucking air in and blowing it out to make the different chords. Cindy lifted her head and howled to the music. Short howls, then long ones, closing her eyes and losing herself in some kind of canine ecstasy that only the mouth organ could induce. My sister's piano playing never had the same effect on her.

Now and again she would have what Mum called 'one of her dos'. She would lose all feeling in her back legs and would try to walk forwards while her rear end careered this way and that trying to follow her. It was disturbing when it first happened. I suppose it was some kind of fit. But if you held her and stroked her, murmuring soothing words, it would pass, and within a few minutes she'd be what Mum called 'as right as ninepence'.

Then there were her lumps. They'd grow here and there. Small, knobbly things underneath the skin of her stomach. The vet seemed unwilling to do anything about them, and they never seemed to trouble her, even if, when a new one appeared every couple of years, we all got a bit concerned. She never did. Concern was not a part of her make-up.

The two of us would go off regularly to the fields down by the river, or to Middleton Woods, but the moors were her favourite place. If she could find a rabbit hole, she would dig happily for hours, and when she showed signs of becoming bored, a quick poke of the soil with your foot a short way back from the entrance would send her into a frenzy of burrowing once more. She was, rather fittingly for a gardener's dog, a born digger.

But there were occasional disasters. Cindy was never one to roam, but her short legs did make her difficult to find among the bracken. Usually you could spot her precise location by the quivering of the fronds overhead, but on one occasion I lost her completely. I called and called, but there was no sign.

I leaped on to the top of a boulder that rose like the back of a hippo three feet into the air above the bracken to get a better view, but the light was fading. It wouldn't be dark for hours yet, but heavy clouds were bowling over the top of the moor. It would be raining before long.

With panic rising inside me, as much at the probable reaction of my mother as the loss of the dog, I wandered slowly downhill, calling all the while, 'Cindy! Come on, girl! Cindy . . .'

To no avail. Nothing, no movement at all, except that of a startled sheep, which leaped bleating from the bracken and frightened me half to death.

I tried to work out a plausible lie. That the dog had spotted something and run off after it, and that try as I might I could not catch up with her. But I knew it wouldn't wash. The dog had gone, that much was clear, but it wasn't my fault. Except that it was. I should have been watching her. And I was being the Lone Ranger at the time, galloping on my horse along the gully known as Rocky Valley, which was the nearest we had to the set of a Hollywood Western on Ilkley Moor. The path was of white silver-sand, and the boulders that towered up on either side of it were a dead ringer for a canyon or a gulch. Whatever a gulch was. I knew it was something you cut people off at, and Rocky Valley looked suitable.

I was wearing my black leather gloves – well, not mine, but those of an elderly aunt who had come to my mother with a box of clothes that were too small for her. They fitted me, and they were thin riding-style gloves with no lining that looked just like the ones the Lone Ranger wore when he handled his silver bullets. My silver bullet was the metal end that had broken off one of Grandad's old walking sticks, and I used to keep it in my pocket, then take it out and roll it round between my leather-gloved fingers murmuring, 'A silver bullet, the only kind the Lone Ranger uses. The lucky silver bullet.'

I took the gloves off and stuffed them in my pocket with the silver bullet, hiding the evidence of my wayward mind.

I ran at first, while I had the energy. Along the path beside the reservoir. Ahead of me, I could see a small, dark figure. As I came closer, I could see that it was a nun. I ran past her and she called out, 'Excuse me?'

Reluctantly I turned back to face her.

'Would you be awfully kind,' she asked, 'and fetch me the cushion from that seat back there?' She pointed up the path – a good hundred yards back – then turned once more to me with a kindly look on her face. I was already late. I nodded, and bolted back up the rough track to the long bench where a black silk cushion rested, forgotten in the nun's haste to be back for prayers at the convent on the edge of the moor.

'Bless you. That's so kind,' she murmured as I handed over the cushion, bowed, which is what I thought you probably had to do to nuns, and then ran on still searching for the missing dog.

I ran down Cowpasture Road and over the railway bridge, my lungs burning, and the pain of a stitch biting into my side. There was no time now to dawdle and wait for the enveloping smoke from one of the engines that would roar underneath, though I'd have been grateful for the time that might have helped me cook up a better story.

Along the edge of Railway Road and down Nelson Road. The tears were not far away now. What if she had been run over? What if she were on her way to Addingham? What if . . . It didn't bear thinking about . . . What if someone had pinched her? No. She was a mongrel. Nothing special. But she was friendly, and good-looking, and . . .

I was not sure what worried me more – the loss of the dog or the prospect of the whalebone hairbrush landing on my bum. It wasn't used often, but tonight, as sure as could be, would be one of them. My father's voice would be raised, then he'd send me up to bed and follow me with the hairbrush. My palms began to sweat as I rounded the corner from the front of the street to the back. I had a sickly feeling in the pit of my stomach. I squeezed the empty dog lead as if somehow, magically, it might bring her back.

I reached the yard and took a deep breath. I would tell them exactly what had happened; I would be totally honest about it and explain how sorry I was, and that the nun had delayed me, and that if they wanted, I would go back up to the moor with a torch and look for her, but that as she was such a small dog, it had been very difficult to watch her all the time with the bracken being long and all that, and I didn't mind going without my tea and my pocket money for the next month, and . . . then I saw the back doorstep.

Cindy was sitting there looking up at the handle. She turned and saw me, then wagged her tail and bounded up to me, licking my legs and making those excited 'Where have you been?' noises that dogs make.

I fell on her neck with relief, and then the back door opened. I looked up. It was my dad.

'You're a bit late. Where've you been?'

'Up on the moors with the dog.'

'Well, you'd better get washed quickly. Your tea's ready.'

'Righto.'

The dog walked to her basket and took a long drink from her bowl.

I washed my hands and sat up at the table.

'Was it nice up there?' asked Mum, cocking her head in the direction of the moors.

'Yes. Fine.' I felt for the gloves in my pocket. They were not there. I'd lost them among the bracken. All that remained was the silver bullet. The lucky silver bullet. That must have been what did the trick.

I ate my dinner at the same time that the nun was probably saying her prayers.

Beyond Otley, Wharfedale becomes more industrial as you edge towards Leeds and Bradford. I went to day-release classes in Shipley on the outskirts of Bradford for my City and Guilds in horticulture, and the bus journey seemed to take for ever. Bradford, we never visited when I was a child. 'It's a bit rough,' said my mother confidentially. Leeds, we would go to on special shopping trips maybe two or three times a year, when Mum needed a new hat or Dad needed a suit. But they seldom ventured beyond the comfort of Schofields. I remember Mum looking wistfully at a shining navy-blue pram when we were in there once. It had gleaming swan-necked chrome handles and new leather suspension straps. It was a Silver Cross – the finest in the land and made locally in Guiseley. 'There's a special deal in here,' she said. 'If you buy your pram in Schofields and tell them what day the baby's due, you get the pram for free if it turns up on the right day.' I suppose the deal was negated in the case of a Caesarian section. And, anyway, it was of academic interest now: Kath and I turned out to be the full brood.

Company

I wasn't aware that we'd had any family discussion about the possibility of an increase in numbers, but then I was only four and a half when Kath arrived, so it might have been mentioned in conversation and I'd not really taken it in. I must have noticed Mum getting bigger – she was very slight.

Several things happened at the birth: I was packed off to Auntie Bee's in Otley for a fortnight, my mum went to her mother's to get help looking after the baby, and my dad went into hospital with pneumonia. Mum would have told him off for attention-seeking – she was never a very patient nurse.

I didn't enjoy my time with Auntie Bee and Uncle Herbert – he was grumpy, and she was impatient. It's funny; in later life she was one of the sweetest-natured, gentlest women I've ever met (and Uncle Herbert was still grumpy).

Their sons, David and Arnold, were slightly older than Kath and me, and kept on a fairly tight rein (though they did have baked beans with their tea, which Mum thought very slack). It's a wonder she let me stay there.

Eventually I was allowed back home – the first few days at Ash Grove, staying with Grandma Hardisty, where my first sight of breasts as my mother fed my sister gave rise to the question 'Is that what them things are for?'

Soon we all moved back to Nelson Road and my dad went back to work for a quiet life.

Despite the age difference, Kath and I got on very well and I fulfilled the usual role of protective brother, in spite of the fact that my mother reckoned my sister had me wrapped round her little finger.

Kath decided I was really quite useful and declined to speak for the first two and a half years of her life – allowing me to do all the talking for her. Only when we took a holiday with Dad's best man in Southampton for a few days did she start to speak for herself – I was too busy looking at the ships to pay much attention. The *Queen Mary* and the *Queen Elizabeth* were both in port during the same week. We saw them from the Isle of Wight ferry. It rained on the Isle of Wight. Mum would never hear a good word for it after that.

It was not long before I realised that boys and girls had a totally different outlook on life. Having got to the age of four and a half as a relatively self-sufficient soul, it began to dawn on me that you couldn't ignore sisters, even for a few minutes. They had to be involved. This was all very well when Kath was prepared to muck in with games of cowboys and Indians, but when I was expected to show an interest in her dolls, I drew the line.

We did have common ground when it came to pets. We both had rabbits. Sisters, they were – she had Wilmer and I had Lulu. We cared for them well, fed them on bran and oats, and they had a five-star hutch courtesy of my dad. They died within a couple of months, while the Dinsdales' rabbit next door – Patchy, ignored from dawn till dusk and from one end of the week to the other – lasted several years. There was no justice in this as far as my sister and I could see, and after that Kath lost heart. I fared a little better with Snowy, the imaginatively named New Zealand white, but even he perished within the year. Only with goldfish did we excel. We got bored with them and as a result Stripey and Peter lived into their twenties, swimming around in a tank of pea soup.

Not all the brothers and sisters in the street got on with one another, but Kath and I rubbed along pretty well most of the time. She was happy to come and play doctors and nurses on the old bed frames down in the saleroom yard, and we'd be taken almost everywhere together – to Auntie Bee's in Otley, where we were allowed to watch *Popeye* on ITV while Mum bridled at the tea table, and to the church social once a year at the Winter Gardens in Ilkley, where Mum and Kath always had new homemade dresses. They were invariably of the same fabric, but different styles. Kath had no shop-bought clothes (apart from underwear and socks) until she went to grammar school.

Not that all our entertainments were so elaborate. We'd still enjoy watching the gasman emptying the meter at the bottom of the cellar steps – ours was grey, for sixpences and shillings; Cookie's, next door, was red for pennies. The meter man wrapped the coins in rolls of paper before putting them into a big Gladstone bag and lumbering off down the street.

We'd have baths together when we were young – it was very unfair: I always got the tap end. And Mum only bought Gibbs Dentifrice toothpaste – a pink or blue block in a tin – which was cheaper than the tubes of SR we were always nagging her to buy. We had to rub our brush on the block until it went frothy.

There would be bedtime stories together – 'Toby Twirl and Eli Phant and Peter Penguin, too, went out to gather blackberries which in abundance grew' and Beatrix Potter and Noddy. Mum was a good reader, with meaningful expression in her voice, even if all her characters did sound the same. Then she'd send me off up to my bedroom in the attic and come a few minutes later to kiss me goodnight and go out leaving the door slightly ajar. The final greeting was always the same: 'Night-night, God bless, peepy-times, see you in the morning . . .' Her footsteps would fade away down the stairs and the vision of Holman Hunt's *Light of the World* would gradually disappear into the gloom in the corner by the window.

Every piece of new domestic equipment seemed to be a land-mark. When we got a fridge – a little three-foot-square one that could only take two pints of milk, some margarine and cheese – she would always forget to take the marge out before spreading it on the bread, so she warmed it up on top of the cream Bakelite radio. One day it melted and the radio blew up.

These memories come like little shafts of light – sparkling briefly and then receding into the gloom. But I do remember the special days in the year – the high days and holidays like Bonfire Night, when part of the vegetable patch would be cleared for a fire, and we'd make a guy out of Dad's old work overalls and jacket. The neighbours would all come up the back to look, and you'd have to see who they were by the light of the bonfire. There would be baked potatoes in their jackets, pushed into the embers as the fire died, and slabs of parkin and beakers of cocoa to keep you warm. Sparklers and golden rain, we were allowed to hold while their vivid showers of sparks shot up into the air, and a Catherine wheel would be nailed to the door of the midden. It never went round properly, and Dad – the only one with fingers tough enough for the job – would be sent to set it spinning again. He never winced, but then his hands were like leather.

Jumping crackers would be let off to make us leap into the air as they crackled and snapped around our feet, and bangers would be tossed into the crowd of onlookers by naughty boys, who were admonished by the mums for being 'daft'.

'Don't do that – you'll have somebody's eye out.' It was always the same threat, and to our continued disappointment, it never once happened.

Our rockets were pathetic – one quick 'whoosh' and they were gone – but what did we expect for sixpence? There were no showers of stars, but if you watched, you could see the small red glow of the spent cardboard tube making its way back to earth. With any luck it would land in our garden, and the following day we could collect them all up – soggy from a night's rain and making our fingers smell of bad eggs and damp gunpowder.

The night before Bonfire Night was feverishly anticipated. It was known as Mischief Night. As soon as it grew dark, we would leave the house, armed with a square of greaseproof paper into which we'd sneaked a spoonful of Lyle's golden syrup. Gleefully Kath and I would round up Janet and Mickey Hudson, Stephen Feather and Philomena Forrest, Virginia and Robert Petty and set off on our mission of mayhem.

Doorknobs would be smeared with the syrup, then we'd knock on doors or ring bells and run and hide. The girls ran off first leaving the boys to do the dirty work and be quick off the mark. It was not enough to ring a doorbell once and disappear; you had to ring it several times until the owner was so exasperated that they came outside and pulled the door closed after them, smearing the syrup on their hands and muttering, 'Little buggers', as they stared out into the night, trying to focus their eyes in the darkened street.

The other trick was to fling people's metal dustbin lids into their backyards, making as much noise as possible. They'd run out to see what was the matter and we'd be hiding behind the wall, hardly daring to breathe.

Only once did I get caught – by Wilf Phillips at the bottom house on the other side of the street.

I'd already lobbed his bin lid over the wall of the yard twice and was starting to feel brave. I sneaked back to do it again, holding my breath and not daring to make a noise. As my hand reached for the lid once more, so Wilf leaped up from the other side of the bin. I let out a yell and ran like hell, my heart thumping in my chest, but he was a good runner, even in his slippers, and caught up with me on the corner of the road and cuffed me round the ear.

'Miserable sod,' said Stephen Feather. 'Why can't he take a joke?'

But we didn't do it again.

Our sports came in seasons – marbles in summer, conkers in autumn and jacks in winter. When the grass down by the river was tall and lush, we'd make squeaking noises by blowing on a single blade, sandwiched between our thumbs. Mickey Hudson had Japanese knotweed growing in his back garden. It made perfect pea-shooters. A packet of dried peas from Thornber's top shop could last us all day.

And then, in Wimbledon fortnight there would be the tennis. Mum's battered pre-war racket would be hauled out from the cellar – bent and buckled by damp – and pressed into service against the bus-garage wall at the bottom of the street on which a white line would be chalked three feet off the ground, and the three chalked wickets rubbed out with spit. Mickey's racket was old, too, but at least it was painted, not wooden like mine. And he had a press.

Stephen Feather, or Fezz, as we called him, was very dismissive. 'I'm getting a new one,' he boasted. 'A Slazenger – from Dobbies and Robbies.'

Dobson and Robinson was the sports shop on the Grove – an Aladdin's cave of Slazenger and Dunlop Maxply Fort rackets as well as rugby balls, football boots and every sporting requisite a young boy could dream of. It smelled of leather and rubber, and sold tennis balls that were white. Ours were all dark grey and didn't bounce very high. Some of them had lost all their wool from being worried by the dog. Still, when we played cricket with them, the ones that did still sport a bit of fluff didn't sting quite as much as a cork ball when you tried to catch them, or caught a side-swipe from Dokey Gell on your cheek.

We admired Fezz's new racket and tried to cover our jealousy, though it was hard not to feel a bit pleased when he misjudged a return and scraped off the paint on the bus-garage wall.

'Aw, me Mum'll kill me!'

We found some white paint in the saleroom yard and touched it up, but I think she noticed. He wasn't allowed out the following night.

Holidays were the times when the family was thrown together – often in the same room. Twice we braved Butlins at Filey – my parents attracted by the fact that it cost £60 all in for the four of us, with them in a double bed at one end of the chalet and Kath and me in bunks at the other. But most years it was Bispham – considered by Mum to be the select end of Blackpool, but not as stuck-up as Lytham St Anne's, which she said was a bit dull.

We never went abroad. Not until I was twenty. I think Mum was nervous of overseas travel with two small children. Mrs Walkinshaw, from the chip shop – who hadn't any teeth – had recently spent a holiday in Spain. Mum was clearly rattled by Mrs Walkinshaw's profligacy and ever afterwards she was known as 'Spain without the teeth', the inference being that she should have got her priorities right and invested in dentures before sunshine.

Pendennis in Hesketh Avenue was our choice of boarding house, run by Mr and Mrs Schofield and Mrs Schofield's mum. Well, Mrs Schofield's mum didn't really run it, but she sat just inside the kitchen door in her floral pinny and dispensed wisdom to all who would listen. Dennis and Joan Petty, next door but one to us in Nelson Road, had said it was clean and economical so we went on their recommendation. Mum and Dad would have a double bed in one room, and my sister and I would have a double in the room next door. There would be one suitcase between the four of us – a blue cardboard one with expanding locks – and a new set of towels each year. Mum had standards.

We'd catch the coach outside Tipping's, the coal merchant's that doubled as a travel agent's in Brook Street, and the journey to Blackpool would take us the best part of the day, with a stop on the way for coffee and squash just over the border in Lancashire.

And when we got back on the coach, did Mum *have* to ask, 'Have you been?' in a voice just loud enough to be overheard?

That night, supper would be a funny sort of meal – a bit of fish for those who had just arrived, and a pot of tea or a glass of milk. Not until the following day would the crate of pop – the Vimto and the despised cream soda – be brought to the table for the children to choose from.

On the first day there were jobs to be done – theatre tickets to be booked for Ken Dodd at the Winter Gardens and tickets for Charlie Cairoli at the Tower Circus. We'd go to the zoo at the Tower if it rained, to see the lion who lived there and looked more bored each year as he paced the cage – three steps and turn, three steps and turn. I dreamed of letting him out. Kath said it wasn't a good idea: there'd be nothing for him to eat in Blackpool – apart from the people.

We'd go to the Tower Ballroom if Reginald Dixon was in residence, and watch him rise up out of the floor to the strains of 'Oh, I do like to be beside the seaside'. Mum and Dad would have a dance or two across the shiny parquet floor, while Kath and I ate biscuits and waited patiently for them to finish.

There were donkey rides on the beach – Nellie and Samson with their names painted on their bridles, each of them far too old and far too wise ever to break into a trot, no matter how hard you dug in your heels.

There were grey-green crabs to be fished for with lumps of bread dangled from string into the boating pool, and occasionally a trip to the Pleasure Beach to see the laughing clowns in the glass case and the big dipper, where groups of young women with their hair in curlers and pink nets would be taken for a ride by cocky-looking Teddy boys with long coats and Brylcreemed hair.

Mum could not see the women who had come out in unsuitable dress without murmuring under her breath, 'Silly dames.' At Butlins they were known as 'misguided misses'.

The women would scream as the carriages hurtled down the track, and the boys would grin gormlessly and hold on with just one hand to impress them. In the evening the curlers would come out and the nets would come off in readiness for a night on the tiles in stilettos and tight-waisted skirts. If you came home late from the theatre or the circus, you could see them tottering back to their digs shrieking with laughter and sometimes throwing up on the prom.

'Don't look,' warned Mum. 'They should know better.'

On sunny days we'd stay on the beach from ten in the morning until late afternoon, and Dad would pretend to fall asleep so that we could bury him in the sand.

As a special treat for being nice to my sister for a whole week, Dad would take me for a boy's night out at the cinema to see a film – *The Guns of Navarone* or *Zulu* – while Mum and Kath did a jigsaw in the silent sitting room behind the net curtains at the front of Pendennis.

'Did you enjoy that, Algy?' Dad would ask when we came out into the fading light.

'Yes. Can we go again?'

'We'll see.'

But we never did. Instead, on the last evening, we'd walk up to the end of the road, cross the promenade and stroll towards Fleetwood and Thornton Cleveleys looking at the illuminations – strings and strings of coloured bulbs blowing in the stiff breeze and reflected in the rain-washed prom, and set pieces with moving parts that shone like jewels in the pitch-black night. Between them all snaked the green-and-cream trams, clanging their way along the tracks and creating their own illuminations on wet nights with a shower of sparks.

Dad would hold my hand to cross the road. It would be softer at the end of the week than the beginning – softened by a week of relaxation and an absence of plumbing. Past shabby kiosks selling 'Kiss me quick' hats and candyfloss, plastic Zorro swords and pirate bandanas, we'd wander wearily back to the digs for a bit of supper – a Rich Tea biscuit and a glass of milk for me, a bottle of Double Diamond for Dad.

This would be the pattern of holidays for most of the folk in our street. Just a week – not a fortnight – and usually at Blackpool or Scarborough, Filey or Brid, as Bridlington was always known. Grannies and older aunties would go to Morecambe or Whitby. Posh people would go to Lytham St Anne's. Cornwall was another country, reserved for those 'up the Grove', and anyway, it would take you a couple of days to get there and then what was left of the week?

All too quickly Saturday morning would arrive and we'd pile back on to the coach for the long journey home with the bursting suitcase and the once-new towels that now smelled of sea and sand.

There was only the one proper holiday every year for Dad, apart from a few days off at Christmas and a day or two at Easter and Whit. For the rest of the time, Kath and I dreamed and Mum and Dad saved. It was worth it for the *Guns of Navarone* and the smell of sea and sand, and the sight of Mum and Dad dancing together like Fred

Astaire and Ginger Rogers across the glossy floor of the Tower Ballroom.

I went back a few years ago, not on holiday, but to work. It was an incongruous *Songs of Praise* from the Pleasure Beach. The kiosks and the candyfloss are unchanged, and the big dipper was still flinging rows of teenagers down its perilous slopes. The music is different now, but the thrill is the same and the girls still scream, even if they don't wear curlers any more.

Comfortingly, some things never change – the smell of fried onions, toffee apples and fish and chips. The sight of donkeys on the rain-soaked sand. The trams still squeak and clang along the prom, and the two laughing clowns were still rollicking in their glass case outside the Pleasure Beach. A few of the boarding houses in Bispham are still hanging on to an air of respectability, by the skin of their teeth, though I doubt that the bottle of Vimto has quite the pull that it used to.

But the Tower Ballroom has lost none of its sparkle. The mighty organ still rises up out of the floor to the strains of 'Oh, I do like to be beside the seaside', though Reginald Dixon and Ernest Broadbent are long gone.

If I sit on the velvet-covered seats that surround the dance floor and half close my eyes, I can see a woman in a homemade peach-coloured brocade dress and a man in a smart grey suit dancing together. She rests the back of her left hand on his right shoulder, and he has his right arm round her narrow waist. She wears suede high-heeled shoes, and he guides her confidently across the ball-room, his feet seeming to slide over the floor without touching it as he manoeuvres her in graceful circles. They only have eyes for one another, and the rest of the holidaymakers dance round them like moths round a flame. Listen carefully and you can catch the tune. He is humming as he dances, and she is smiling in that contented way she has when he holds her. The organ is not its usual ebullient self. It is softer now, more gentle, and the words come floating from somewhere up on the balcony – 'When I grow too old to dream, I'll have you to remember . . .'

The station is at the very centre of Ilkley – at the top of Brook Street – and until Dr Beeching wielded his axe, you could travel both eastwards and westwards out of the town. Now you can only go to Leeds and Bradford.

I got up at four in the morning one day in the mid-1960s to see the old iron railway bridge taken down by a crane. That day the view from the top of Brook Street to the distant woods of Middleton was opened up for the first time in a century. We should have been grateful for the improvement, but there was an air of sadness about it all, not least because now we were only connected to two industrial towns, rather than to Skipton – the 'Gateway to the Dales' – and all stations onwards to the west coast of Lancashire and the Lake District.

In the 1960s, if you hadn't got a car, you were stuck, unless you were prepared to wait for the bus, and they took hours. But in the 1950s, the railway could take you wherever you wanted to go.

To Catch a Train

'Quick! It's comin'!'

I was at the bottom of the steps of the railway bridge when my sister called. Dawdling again. Looking at some crummy wild flower – a bit of jack-by-the-hedge growing in a crevice of the pavement, or convolvulus, snaking its way through the rusty chain-link fencing alongside the track to open its milky-white trumpets that everybody seemed to hate. I thought it was spectacular, especially when it grew over the fence at the bottom of our garden. Dad hated it. Bindweed, he called it. Said its roots were 'bloomin' impossible to get rid of'. I wondered why he didn't give up and just leave it.

Kath's voice was more insistent now: 'Ala! You'll miss it!'

I left the bindweed to twine away without me and hared up the wooden steps of the sparkly silver-grey footbridge that crossed the railway line just outside the station. The roar was louder now – a deep-throated 'chuff-chuff-chuff', backed by a kind of thundery growl. I had to sprint the last few yards across the wobbly wooden boards, but just made it in time to see my sister disappear from view in an enormous cloud of grey-white smoke as the engine roared underneath us.

We held our breath to avoid breathing in the mixture of coal dust, smoke and steam, but not always successfully; then we coughed ourselves silly for a few minutes and wiped our watering eyes. We'd be in trouble for the smuts on our clothes – 'Have you been on that bridge again?' – but it was worth it.

It was thrilling and terrifying at the same time – the loudest noise we ever heard, and the nearest you could come to the kind of danger that would make your heart beat faster. It wasn't surprising that half the boys in the class wanted to become engine drivers. There was even one, Johnny Williams, the only lad in the school as small as me, who still wanted to be an engine driver when they switched to diesels, but then he was a hard case.

I had my Ian Allan trainspotter's book in which the numbers were methodically ticked off, but I could never share with Johnny his passion for standing on a draughty station platform and – with a ruler, mind, not freehand – scoring through the numbers once he had spotted the train. They weren't even particularly interesting numbers – 45393, that sort of thing. My little paperback book with the steaming locomotive on the front was full of them. Johnny's was full of neatly Biroed lines.

But the trains themselves would always excite. Before we boarded the train to Leeds or, in summer when trips to the west coast were on the cards, to Skipton where we'd change for Morecambe, I'd walk down to the front to take a look at the steaming engine. It would sit there like an animal just waiting to leap into action – hot water dribbling from it like saliva, and steam spurting with alarming un-predictability from under cowls and cylinders and out of copper pipes.

A peep into the cab would reveal two black-faced and sweating men in faded blue overalls and peaked caps that seemed to be made out of tar, shovelling coal into the furnace or leaning on the thick black door drinking tea out of enamel mugs.

'Can I come up, mister?' I'd ask, but the answer would always be the same – 'Nay, lad, we're not allowed. But can you see the fire?'

They'd open the door of the furnace and I'd stare at the flames inside – so hot they were almost white. I nodded. 'I want to be an engine driver.'

'Aye, but you're nobbut a lad.'

'When I grow up I mean.'

White teeth would smile out of the soot-blackened face. 'We'll see. You might think differently then.'

They didn't seem to realise they had the best job in the world.

Now it was my mother's turn to be impatient. 'Come on, Sparrow, or it'll go without us.'

She'd hold open the thick and heavy door, while Kath and I climbed into the compartment, then pull it shut with a startling bang that seemed to shake the entire train. The thick leather strap would be tugged inwards to raise the window a little, and then slipped over the brass stud so that the window was always slightly ajar. Just as the back door of the house was always open, so the window of the train compartment was never entirely closed, even in the worst of weathers.

'How long will it take?'

'Less than an hour. Here you are.' She'd reach into her wicker shopping basket and pull out a copy of *Robin* for my sister and *The Children's Newspaper* for me. I didn't really like it. There were no colour pictures and it was a bit boring, but it was meant to improve my education. On the way home, I might be allowed a copy of *Swift* – midway in maturity between *Robin* and *Eagle*.

When I got bored, I'd read the adverts in the compartment. 'Mum, what's a laxative?'

'Why do you want to know?'

''Cos it says up there.' I nodded in the direction of the advert.

'It helps you go when you can't.'

'How?'

'It just does.'

'What do you do with it?'

'You drink it.'

'The whole bottle?'

'No. You'd be in trouble if you did.'

'Why?'

'Look, why don't you just read your newspaper, we'll be there soon.'

But I was bored with my newspaper, and it seemed to me that Mum and Dad were sometimes a bit impatient of my questions if, as they said, they bought the newspaper to help improve my education; to make me more curious. Dad had got quite irritated when I'd asked him what a midwife was. He said I'd already asked him once. I couldn't remember. I must have forgotten.

I looked out of the window at the trains – they were much more exciting, especially when one thundered by on the track right next to us.

The carriages themselves were cream at the top and maroon at the bottom, and, inside, the compartments were panelled with dark wood. There was a mirror for Mum to check her hair in before we got off, and a knotted string rack for luggage. The seats had really strong springs that you could bounce on when Mum wasn't looking. They smelled funny, though, and if you hit one hard, it would release a cloud of dust that would glint in the shafts of sunlight that shone in through the window.

If the wind was in the right direction, some of the smoke would blow in from the engine. When it did, Mum would pull the window up on the offending side and lower the other one, in between reading her romance. Mum read romances with pink and pale-blue covers, and Dad read Westerns written by people with funny names like Shane and Clint. *The Cruel Sea* was on our small bookshelf at home, but I never saw him read it. There was also a book called *The Knave of Diamonds* by Ethel M. Dell, which Mum told me never to touch 'because it isn't suitable for a boy'. I took it down one day when she was out, but I couldn't find anything remotely exciting between its covers. I decided she was right.

When Dad came with us, in between reading his Western, he'd look out of the window with me to see if we could see any interesting trains – what Johnny Williams called 'namers'. Sometimes they would be painted dark green or maroon and they looked much smarter than the sooty black jobs that did the usual run to Leeds and back with carriages or freight.

The longest journey we ever did was to London when we went to Southampton to see Dad's best man. We swapped trains at Leeds and Dad heaved the single expanding case up on to the luggage rack while Mum handed round the magazines and books. *The Children's Newspaper*, she knew, would not be enough to see me through this journey, so there was a colouring book, too, and a book all about transport. On the back page of this book, which I had had for about a year now, was a picture of an engine that had become my favourite. It had sleek lines, was painted in a unique shade of sky blue, and was called *Mallard*.

'Do you think we'll see it on the way?' I asked Dad.

'I don't know, Algy. We might. It runs on the Leeds to London line.'

'We might, then?'

'We might. But not for long – it's the quickest train there is. I think it holds the record.'

'What for?'

'Going fast.'

'Where to?'

'Anywhere.'

Mum settled down with her romance, Dad with his Western, and Kath with *Robin*. I remained glued to the window for mile after mile. To no avail. There was not the merest sniff of *Mallard*. I looked again at the picture of the sleek engine on the back of the book and sighed.

'How long will it take?'

Dad looked up. 'A long time yet.'

The egg sandwiches came out around Derby. And the Thermos flask of milky coffee with the greaseproof paper round the cork that had replaced the lost stopper.

Then there was an apple. And a Penguin biscuit. And then there was nothing to do but go on looking.

Five hours later we pulled into King's Cross.

'At least we're not late,' murmured Dad. But there was still no sign of *Mallard*.

'Never mind, Algy.' Dad lifted me up on to his knee. 'Perhaps we'll see it on the way back.'

I wasn't hopeful, and I didn't fancy another five hours of gazing out of a grimy window in the hope of a one-second glimpse of the fastest train in the country.

Dad heaved the case down from the luggage rack, and Mum helped Kath and me down on to the platform. Weary and disappointed, I trailed after Dad, who was now well into his customary holiday walk – the lopsided one with the heavy case in one hand and the tickets and the mac in the other, his flat cap tilted over his right eye.

As we neared the front of the train, we could see the clouds of steam and smoke that billowed from our equally weary engine, and as they cleared and the locomotive became more visible, Dad put down his case and said, 'Well, I'll be jiggered!'

There, in front of us, was *Mallard*, spitting and sighing and pausing for breath. The reason we had not seen her was that she was pulling us.

I don't remember saying anything at all. Just staring at the sky-blue engine with its sloping black front, and the cab that seemed to be high up in the air. I waved at the driver and he waved back and gave me a wink. Then he looked at his watch and shouted down, 'Quick enough for you?'

'Yes, thank you.'

I told Johnny Williams about it when I got back.

'*Mallard?*'

'Yes.'

'Pulled you to London?'

'Yes.'

'Lucky bugger.' And then he went on scoring lines through the numbers he'd logged that weekend: 45394, 45395 . . .

I've always preferred letters to numbers myself.

From up on the moors, I can see Addingham away to the left (whose pubs stayed open a full half-hour after those in Ilkley closed), and just round the bend in the valley, and further up it, is the market town of Skipton, 'the Gateway to the Dales' – a claim that has always irritated me. The implication being that Ilkley hasn't quite made it inside. Between Skipton and Ilkley are the villages of Burnsall and Bolton Abbey, Grassington and Kettlewell, Appletreewick and Barden – all of them beauty spots to be visited on Sunday afternoons once Dad had got a van and could take us out on a 'run'.

'Come on, Algy. And bring the cushions.' The cushions were snatched from the settee for me and my sister to sit on in the back of the second van we had – a Mini pick-up. There was room only for Dad and Mum in the front of this one. Kath and I sat with our backs to the cab under the canvas awning that kept off the worst of the weather, but sucked in most of the exhaust fumes. There were no seat belts; we just steadied ourselves with our arms when he went round a corner a bit fast.

Domestic Offices

B arring the flowering currant bush outside the back door, which
Dad cut into an orderly cube each summer for fear it should get
'out of hand', the garden at the back of Nelson Road was Mum's
domain. Not that she was especially adventurous. Outside the back
door, the bikes would lean against the house wall under an old pram
cover or a bit of threadbare stair carpet. The rough lane known as
the back would be crossed to reach the garden, which was up a few
steps on the other side of a broken gate attached to the midden – the
stone-built shed with a split barn door covered in flaking maroon
paint. It must, originally, have been the outside toilet, though the
house did have indoor sanitation when we arrived. This original use
would make sense of the fact that we never used it, even for storage,
and that as kids we were banned, by Mum, from even opening the
door. Whenever we were emboldened to enquire why it was out of

bounds, she'd say there was a particularly nasty sort of spider in there and that if you went in, you would probably catch a disease. I was always a bit wary of it. My mother's warnings clearly had the desired effect.

The garden would have won no prizes for design. There was a rectangle of grass ('lawn' would be too grand a word) that was cut with a clanking side-wheeled lawnmower on Saturday afternoons in the summer, when Dad came home from work at noon. There was never a grass box, so clippings were forever being brought into the house.

'Who's come in without wiping their feet?' my mother would wail, shaking out the rag rug into the yard. The garden was primarily a place to stand the pram, and where washing could be dried on the line that was held up with a long wooden prop. Monday was washing day, when the peggy tub would be pulled out, the house would be filled with steam and the smell of starch and soapsuds, and Mum would bash the dirt out of Dad's collars and navy-blue overalls with the help of a washboard and elbow grease. Until we got the washer.

It was a single tub with an agitator in the side, but you could plug it in and let it do the bashing of the collars for you (once you'd rubbed a bit of Fairy soap on them for added cleanliness). It stood in the middle of the kitchen floor and bubbled away under its smart aluminium lid for the duration of the wash. Then Mum would switch it off and haul out the sodden clothes, dashing with them to the sink, where they'd be rinsed, while the washer itself was emptied via the length of hose attached to it into a bucket. The trick was to

get the clothes into the clean water in the sink at the same time as the washer was emptying without letting the bucket overflow.

Sweat would pour down Mum's brow from under the scarf that was fastened round her head.

'Pull the pipe out, Sparrow – it's nearly full!'

I'd hold up the pipe so that no more water would flow, and learned, at my mother's knee, before I went to school, the siphoning principle.

All the women in the street would do their washing on the same day, and to get back home from school you'd have to duck under row after row of sheets and pillowcases, shirts and socks, and the hefty knickers of elderly ladies who lived on their own. We had a lot of them, but the one we knew best was Cookie, who lived next door.

It was Cookie who came to the rescue on the day of the disaster, but she came too late.

At the age of three or four, mobile but still relatively unsteady, I reached up to the kitchen worktop to grab a handle that I could see from below. It was the handle of a coffee pot. It was full and, deaf to my mother's cry to leave it alone, I pulled it towards me. It came and so did the contents – boiling-hot milky coffee streamed down my right side.

In a fit of panic Mum rushed to the sink, pulled off my shirt and grabbed a towel, which she wrapped round me.

'Cookie, Cookie!' she cried through the open back door.

'What is it, duck?' The old lady bustled in.

'He's just scalded himself – what do I do?'

'Get him to the Coronation, duck.'

The Coronation Hospital was a mile away on the other side of the railway, but I was dashed there with all speed – over the railway bridge and up the lane.

The doctor shook his head. 'Who put the towel on him?'

My mother confessed.

'Worst thing you could have done. It'll take the skin off.'

And it did. In one large sheet. I still bear the scars below my right arm. After siphoning, lesson number two was that you don't put fabric on a scald. Cold water is better.

Ilkley itself lies immediately below the moor. At its heart is Brook Street, the main north–south thoroughfare, lined with shops. It has a flower-filled traffic island at the top. I used to help plant it up with geraniums in summer and wallflowers in autumn. The traffic doesn't go very fast in Brook Street; it can't because there are always dozens of people trying to cross. It's only a couple of hundred yards long, and the brook runs beneath it now, channelled from its exit from the moor until it relieves itself into the Wharfe just by the riverside toilets. As kids, we used to stand above the rusty metal grid that marked the beck's outfall into the river, wondering if it really was the water that had come from the moor or the water that had come from . . . somewhere else entirely.

'They must be bloody big fish in this part of the river,' mused Mickey Hudson.

'Why?' I asked.

'Stands to reason. All that stuff coming out of the bog. They must be bloody enormous.' I try not to feel uneasy when I eat local trout.

Out the Back

Our back garden wasn't the most well-endowed nature reserve, but at least it was handy. The patch of ground at the top of the four old stone steps was, I suppose, about fifteen feet by forty feet. There was an old sycamore tree at the far end, deformed by years of careless pruning, and below it, on the rusted wire netting, 'Dorothy Perkins' did her best to brighten up the month of June.

A narrow border ran round the patch of threadbare grass that had been allowed to take over what once was a vegetable patch. For six or seven years Brussels sprouts and a few potatoes grew in the dusty black earth, until my dad lost the inclination to grow his own, and the Brussels lost the will to live. Only a hydrangea provided some kind of deliberate ornament; the 'Esther Read' daisies and the montbretia weren't so much deliberate as persistent – planted there by some Victorian gardener, they had now dug in their heels and refused to budge.

'Can I have a bit?' I asked.

'Which bit do you want?' asked Mum, whose preserve the garden had now become.

'It doesn't matter. I just want to sow some seeds.'

'Well, you'll have to look after it, mind. I don't want you forgetting all about it, because I know what'll happen – I'll end up doing it.'

I didn't forget all about it. But my dad did. I was given a patch about three feet square. I forked it over and raked it flat, then I went to Woolworth's and looked at the packets of seeds – Cuthbert's and Bees. Somehow Cuthbert's seemed a puny sort of brand name, so I plumped for the more reliable-sounding Bees. I chose a single packet of bright-coloured Livingstone daisies; took them home, sprinkled

135

them on the patch and raked them in. I stuck an old wooden lollipop stick through the bottom of the empty packet, and pushed it in alongside my very first seedbed, like the pictures I'd seen in Beatrix Potter books. An obliging shower of rain resulted in early germination, and I went out to admire my new clutch of seedlings. Perfect. Shimmering in green and crimson, with little sparkly silver bits all over tiny leaves.

I went out to look at them every day for a week. By Saturday a gust of wind had taken away the packet that marked the spot, and the seedlings now looked quite different: they had a boot print in the middle of them. The Livingstone daisies around the outside of the boot print grew well, and eventually covered up the bare patch in the centre where my dad had stepped on what he thought was bare earth.

The liking for plants grew out of a love of nature in general. Every March I'd go up to the tarn on the edge of the moor and fish out some frog spawn. It would live in a jam jar on the windowsill, and I'd watch the sago pudding dotted with full stops that turned first into commas, and then into tiny black tadpoles with gills like miniature antlers.

Soon they would outgrow the jam jar and have to be moved into a goldfish bowl, where they would grow little legs and their tails would slowly shrink.

'They need to eat, you know,' cautioned Mum.

'What do they eat? Goldfish food?' I knew its value. Our two goldfish, Stripey and Peter, lived well into their twenties on one pinch of fish food a week and a once-yearly clean-out. People made the mistake, said my mother, of feeding them too much and cleaning them out too often. While the eventual age of our goldfish did, to some extent, vindicate her claim, it would have been nice to have seen a bit more of them through clearer water.

'No. Tadpoles don't eat fish food. You need to give them meat.'

I looked at the tiny black blobs with their wriggling tails. They did not look like carnivores.

'Hang on.' Mum went to the kitchen worktop and cut a tiny cube of meat from the chunks she was cutting up for stew.

'I read it somewhere. You've got to tie this to a piece of cotton and hang it over the side of the bowl so that it dangles in the water.'

And that's what I did. The tadpoles seemed only vaguely interested, but then there was no sign of any teeth. I couldn't work out how they could draw from it any kind of sustenance. And yet they grew. The question was, what to do with them next?

In the early years we would take them back to the tarn when they had clearly outgrown the house. But when Mum and Dad bought the TV in 1958, I discovered a programme called *Out of Doors*. Once a week, in *Children's Hour*, it looked at what was happening in the outside world at that particular time of year. It was a nature diary, aimed at interesting the young in what went on all around them.

The series gave rise to a book in 1959, and on page 56, in the section devoted to April, was a small article by a man called Leslie Jackman on 'Making a Vivarium'.

'Da-a-ad?'

'Yes?' He spoke from behind his *Daily Express*, as usual.

'Will you make me a vivarium?'

'A what?'

'A vivarium. It's for keeping frogs in. Look . . .'

I offered him the book, and he read, as I did, the opening sentence: 'This is the month when you will almost certainly want to keep a few frogs or toads, so why not make a small vivarium.'

He sighed, said, 'Mmm,' and went back to his paper.

I read on: 'All you need is a wooden box from the grocer's. Knock out one side and nail on an edging of wood measuring one inch by one inch. This will form a surface on which to bed the glass front.'

It all seemed very complicated. I could probably get the wooden box from Mickey Hudson's dad, and we had old broken panes of glass stacked behind the midden, but I'd probably break the glass if I tried to make it fit the box. I read on and dreamed . . . 'A two-inch layer of garden soil mixed with peat . . . a small glass or earthenware bowl to act as a pond . . . Visit a nearby marsh or river and dig up a few roots of rush, sedge, water mint and other waterside plants . . . and so turn it into a home for frogs.'

Dad continued to read his paper, but the following day when I came home from school, there was a vivarium sitting in the backyard – freshly made from a wooden box, with a glass front and even a sliding glass roof. I did like my dad.

He was never overly demonstrative when it came to outward signs of affection towards me – apart from the ruffling of my hair when I sat on the floor in front of his chair to watch telly. He gave me a peck on the cheek to say goodnight when I was little, but that faded out before I achieved double figures. I suppose that like most northern men he was wary of turning his lad into 'a bit of a nancy'. But he showed his affection in other ways – mainly with his ability to make things. Before the vivarium, Father Christmas had brought me the garage for the Dinky toys, the fort with the dozen lead soldiers and the zoo with the lions and tigers and giraffes. The zoo was his *pièce de résistance* – it was made of wood, painted red and yellow and had sliding panels at the back to put the animals in their cages – cages that had real metal bars. It measured about two feet square, with half a dozen cages, and was presided over by a big, fat zookeeper with a top hat and a walking stick.

Dad spent a lot of time in the cellar on November and December evenings. At that time of year it was placed out of bounds to us children. We never realised why. Nor why it was suddenly OK for us to go down there and bring the coal up again on Christmas morning. Wafting up the cellar steps would be the smell of newly sawn timber as well as coal, and a neat pile of wood shavings and sawdust would be heaped in a corner. And still we never rumbled.

He would watch as I discovered the fort or the zoo or the garage in front of the fireplace on Christmas morning. 'Is it all right, Algy?' he'd ask, his eyes glowing every bit as brightly as my own.

'It's wonderful,' was about as much as I could manage, hardly able to believe I had something so special. I must have known they were homemade, and yet I cannot recall ever thanking him in person. Only saying thank you to Santa, as my mother insisted. Perhaps the 'game' was such a tradition that it would have been unkind to have suggested that the toys came from Dad and not from Father Christmas. Perhaps it was to protect my sister – almost five years younger – from the truth. I cannot remember; all I know is that in my heart I felt deep gratitude towards my father.

The homemade toys and carts and vivariums were his way of 'doing his bit' for his children. Money might be in short supply, but he had his hands and the ability to work with them, and then my mother would step in when it came to the more artistic finishing touches – curtains for Kath's doll's house or covers for the pram.

For the vivarium, Mum had found a cut-glass sugar bowl she didn't use (never had frogs such a high-class pond) and an hour down by the river yielded the water plants they spoke of on *Out of Doors*.

Every year from then on we had baby frogs in the vivarium, each and every one of them called Gladys. It was Mum's idea. I just went along with it.

If tadpoles and frogs occupied the early part of the year, then other forms of nature took over in summer. Birds in particular. My constructional skills did stretch as far as making a bird table – from the bottom of an old doll's house that had fallen apart. All it took was one nail to fasten it to the end of a broom handle, and a large hammer to knock it into a soft piece of ground. On top of it, I piled stale bread and handfuls of Swoop wild bird food that I'd persuaded Mum to buy from the pet shop. I even joined something called the Swoopers' Club by sending off a competition form on the back of the packet. The trouble was, I wasn't sure I'd got all the answers right. Did a blackbird run, jump or hop? Did robins eat insects or seeds? To make sure, I filled in several forms and became, as a result, a Swooper four times over.

To ascertain the truth about the blackbird, I watched carefully from the kitchen window when our local one came down to feed. But we were too far away. The garden was beyond the back and I couldn't tell with confidence the precise gait of the distant bird.

So I devised a cunning plan. Armed with a handful of Swoop and an old blackout curtain that my mother now used as a dust sheet when she was decorating, I ventured into the garden one sunny morning in the school holidays.

I scattered the handful of seed on the lawn, then settled down under the big black curtain barely three feet away from it, peering out through a hole. I waited and waited. For ten minutes nothing happened, but my patience was rewarded and I saw the blackbird run, then jump towards the seed. It might even have given a small hop for good measure. The question remained unanswered, but the pleasure of watching wildlife at close quarters amply repaid the discomfort I suffered from the heat of the summer sun under a big black shroud of cloth.

'What's he doing?' Cookie would ask, peering through our kitchen window while she sat on a buffet and drank her elevenses with my mum.

'Birdwatching.'

'Well, he won't see much there, will he?'

'He's got a bird book,' said Mum defensively. 'Ticks things off in it.'

'What sort of things?'

'Sparrows and chaffinches. A few blue tits. A blackbird.'

Cookie harrumphed. 'He should join the naturalists.'

'I think he's a bit young for that.'

'They might take him. I'll talk to Bert Flood.'

Cookie was as good as her word. She did talk to Mr Flood, and in 1959 I became the youngest member of the Wharfedale Naturalists' Society.

I'm still not entirely certain whether or not my mother thought it would involve me taking all my clothes off.

I was never going to be an intellectual. I was bright enough later on in life – reasonably intelligent if not academic – but in the early years I was a slow developer. I did, though, have two facilities that I have always found useful – tenacity and aptitude. Or, put another way, I was determined and good with my hands. Well, I see little point in being able to understand pure maths and quantum physics if you can't hang a cupboard. I might not have the appetite to get through Stephen Hawking's A Brief History of Time, *but I could build you a shelf to put it on.*

Let me loose on something I'm passionate about and I can go at it like a terrier. It's always been that way.

Arts and Crafts

J ohn Brown was good at knitting. I could never see the fascination in 'knit one, purl one'. He'd sit there, with his brow furrowed under his mop of perfectly combed dark-brown hair, wearing his pale-blue jumper, and turn out yard after yard of scarf. And it wasn't even that cold. But Mrs Rishworth seemed pleased with him.

I preferred other forms of craft. I was quite good at sticking things together – bits of paper on to card, that sort of thing – but it never seemed to impress her much.

I was better at home. I'd seen a picture in a magazine about how you could make miniature gardens in old 78-rpm records. All you had to do was put the record in hot water and it would become bendy. Then you pulled up the sides, away from the centre, and as the record cooled it turned into a wavy-edged bowl complete with drainage hole in the base. Quite a few people got a miniature garden for Christmas that year. I think they were a bit surprised.

I was especially good at making model theatres. One came in the form of a multicoloured cut-out book from Pollock's in London. That was the Christmas I got my electric train. To my father's dismay it remained parked in the siding all day while I made the theatre from the one-shilling-and-sixpenny book.

Other theatres, and even television studios with miniature cameras and scenery, I made from cardboard and balsa wood, bought from the *Hobbies Annual*. It was a treasure trove of delights, the *Hobbies Annual* – packed with everything from dolls' house kits to electric motors and steam engines. I would pore over its pages in bed and work out what elaborate constructions I could make, if only I had half-a-crown pocket money instead of a shilling.

But one day Mrs Rishworth came up with an idea that would allow me to compete with John Brown.

'Children! Now, put down your pens and listen.'

She turned away from the blackboard with its carefully written chalk letters – 'f's with big loops and 'r's that looked like staples gone wrong – and peered imperiously through her rimless spectacles, enunciating every word as clearly as she always did.

'We are going to have a competition.'

'What sort of competition, miss?' asked Peter Earle from the back row.

'If you will allow me to continue, I shall tell you.'

'Oh. Right, miss. Sorry, miss.'

'There will, in fact, be two competitions. The first will be for peg dolls . . .'

'Peg whats, miss?'

'PEG DOLLS!'

'Where do you get them, miss?'

'If you will listen, Peter Earle, I will explain.'

'Yes, miss. Sorry, miss.'

Mrs Rishworth drew herself up to her full height – and she was not small. Her ample matron's bosom heaved under her thick red cardigan and white blouse. The pearls at her neck glistened as she spoke.

'Clothes pegs like these . . .' at this point she bent down and picked one up from her desk '. . . with the aid of small scraps of material and coloured pencils can be turned into dolls like these . . .' She took from her desk drawer a small doll that appeared to be one of the wise men from the nativity – with a crown and a flowing robe. She carefully lifted up the robe to reveal the two wooden 'legs' of the peg.

Somebody wolf-whistled. Mrs Rishworth pretended not to notice.

'You can make any kind of doll you wish, and there will be a prize for the best one.'

'Where do we get the pegs, please, miss?' asked John Brown, his mind ever on the domestic.

'I shall give you each a peg and you can bring them back when they are finished. You have the summer holidays to make them so I should get thinking now about what your doll will be.'

Johnny Williams said he was going to make an engine driver. The girls started talking about ball gowns. I didn't know what to make. The hubbub rose.

'Now what did I say?' boomed Mrs Rishworth once more.

'That we have to bring them back after the holidays . . .'

'Yes, and I also said that we would have two competitions. The second will be for something to do with nature. Can you guess what?'

There was a momentary silence before Ian Gledhill said, in his deep and unenthusiastic voice, 'Pets?'

'No. Not pets. We are going to have a competition for pressed flowers.'

At this John Brown brightened and Peter Earle slumped forward on his desk and muttered, 'Aw, bloody hell!'

Mrs Rishworth brought her selective hearing into play, and one of the girls got her out of a spot by asking, 'How do we press them?'

'I shall show you.' (There were lots of 'I shall's from Mrs Rishworth. She was not an 'I will' sort of lady.)

She took a newspaper from the shopping basket by her chair, opened it out and laid it on her desk. Then she removed a buttercup from the jam jar on the windowsill behind her and laid it carefully on top of the paper.

'Spread out the flower into a pleasing shape, then fold over the newspaper like this . . .' She folded the paper so that the buttercup was sandwiched between the two layers. 'Now then, you can place more flowers folded between newspaper on top of this one, and then put them all underneath a rug in your house.'

147

It was fortunate that these were the days before fitted carpet or, as Peter Earle might have put it, we'd have been buggered.

'It really is as simple as that. And then, when your flowers are dry – after about a week – you can take them out of the paper and stick them into an album like this . . .' From her other desk drawer, she pulled what looked like a stamp album, but when she opened it, we could see that different wild flowers had been stuck to every page. There was an audible gasp from the room. Even Peter Earle was impressed.

'How do we stick them in?' asked John Brown quietly.

'I'm glad you asked that, John.'

He could not resist a smug smile as he wriggled in his seat and looked at the floor.

'With stamp hinges. Instead of folding them as you normally do to stick your stamps into your album, just lick them and use them to fasten the stems to the pages. You'll find that a sheet of tissue paper will prevent the pages from sticking together.'

She said 'tissue' properly – with two 's's – unlike her pupils, who would call it 'tishoo'.

At that moment, the sonorous clanging of the handbell signalled that the school day was over, and we all traipsed outside, picking up a peg on the way with Mrs Rishworth's instructions ringing in our ears. 'The pressed flowers and the peg dolls will need to be handed in at the end of the summer holidays. On the first day of the new term.'

I took care to explain things properly when I got home. If I only told Mum 'half a tale', I'd be in trouble, or she'd go down to the school and ask for clarification. With images of rugs and newspaper and stamp hinges whirring around in my head, I spilled out the instructions.

'An album of pressed flowers? By the end of the summer?'

'Yes.'

'Well, I suppose it'll keep you out of mischief.'

And it did. That summer we invested in a wild-flower book to help with identification. We went through the woods, along the riverbank and on the moors collecting flowers and bringing them home to press. On Sunday walks we stopped by promising-looking hedgerows and unpromising-looking waste ground.

I would go off in one direction, while Mum dragged Kath in the other. She was nothing if not committed.

Week after week I laid my wild flowers in newspaper, and the rag rug between the kitchen and the front room became as high as a doorstep – you had to climb up on to it to get from one room to another.

Night after night I would sit up, writing their names in the album in my childish, spidery script with a Platignum fountain pen, having stuck their fuse-wire-thin stems first to my fingers and finally to the rough grey pages of the album with the thin and flyaway stamp hinges. If anyone coughed while I was sticking them in, I'd have to frantically scrabble underneath the table for lost hinges. We found them, years afterwards, underneath the lino and down the sides of the settee.

Mum made most of our bread, but when she needed an extra loaf at the weekend, she would buy one from Hardingham's bakery in Brook Street and I would carefully remove the tissue paper and lay it flat between the pages of my album. As a result, all my flowers – the vetches and the hawkbits, the fox and cubs and the evergreen alkanet, the cow parsley and the water blobs – all smelled of fresh bread.

By the end of the summer I had a collection to be proud of. One or two of them were short of names – nondescript plants with green oval leaves and tiny white flowers – the plant equivalent of 'little brown jobs' in the bird world, but the majority were readily identifiable and clearly named.

On the weekend before we were due to go back to school, I suddenly remembered.

'Mum! We've forgotten the peg doll.'

'What peg doll?'

'The peg doll that has to be done with the pressed flowers.'

Mum frowned. 'You didn't say anything about a peg doll.'

'I did, I did! I'm sure I did.' The panic began to rise. 'Well, I think I did.'

I saw the look in Mum's eye and ran upstairs to my bedroom. Hanging behind the door on a hook was my pump bag – the homemade one with Mum's handwritten name tag on it. It had been there since the end of term – I had no need of pumps during the summer holidays as sandals with the toes cut out were my regulation footwear in August.

I took down the bag and tipped the contents on to the floor – one pair of black elasticated pumps, one tattered school timetable and a small wooden peg.

I scooped it up and walked slowly down the stairs. Mum didn't say anything as I lifted the peg on to the kitchen worktop and gently laid it down. I went to get a drink of water from the sink – to avoid her eye as much as anything.

Then she said brightly, 'Do you have any ideas, then? About this peg doll?'

I could have hugged her. It meant that Mum had gone into rescue mode. She was going to help, and it was not going to be a crisis. She would make sure of that.

'Let me see what I've got by the machine.'

Mum's sewing machine was her most prized possession. In the early days it was a hand-wound Singer, but now she had a treadle version she worked with her feet, which meant that she could have both hands free while the needle went to work – it made it easier to feed the cloth through. It stood under the front window, and beside it was a cloth bag full of remnants – bits of cloth too small to make a garment but too big to throw away.

She rummaged for a while and then straightened up. 'No. Nothing there that inspires.'

My heart sank.

'Just a minute. I think I've got some crêpe paper in the cupboard. Left over from Christmas.'

The tall grey cupboard built into one side of the fireplace was an Aladdin's cave. My sister and I were too small to see into it, which, from my parents' point of view, was probably quite useful. Mum pulled open the door and began her search. She came out with bits of red and green crêpe paper, a tube of Uhu, some pieces of cardboard and a box of crayons – probably intended as a Christmas present for some nephew or niece but never handed out.

Then she went to the sewing-machine drawer and took out a pair of scissors. 'These aren't my dressmaking scissors, mind! I don't want you ever using those.'

I shook my head. 'What are you going to do?'

Mum looked at the clock. 'Good gracious, is that the time? Go on, you get off to bed. I'll start it tonight and then you can help me finish it off tomorrow.'

I kissed her goodnight and left her, as on so many evenings when my dad was out, hunched over her sewing machine, but this time with cardboard and crêpe paper, glue and crayons, rather than floral prints and cotton.

There was no doubt about it, this was a class peg doll. It was propped up on the mantelpiece when I came down in the morning. It was a golliwog wearing a boater and playing a banjo.

'*The Black and White Minstrels* was on last night. It gave me an idea.'

I looked at the beaming doll – its bright-red lips, white eyes and black face sticking out above a green crêpe-paper jacket and red trousers, both beautifully tailored. A pipe cleaner had been wrapped round it for arms, and the banjo was made out of cardboard and stuck on with glue. It was, quite simply, a work of art.

'But you've finished it,' I exclaimed, turning the doll round in my hand.

'Well, I thought I might as well, Sparrow. You've spent so much time on your pressed flowers I don't think they'll mind.'

The following morning I took in the two albums that comprised my pressed-flower collection, taking care that the bread paper did not blow out on the way, and I slipped the peg doll carefully into my pocket.

There was the usual buzz on the first day back at school – swapped stories of holidays in Filey and Brid and Blackpool from those of us on the eastern side of town, and of trips to Scotland and Cornwall for those from the west.

When Mrs Rishworth came into our new classroom (we had all gone up a year) to look at the fruits of our summer labours, she wandered down the long row of albums and murmured, 'Well, some of you have been busy.'

Like the albums, the peg dolls had been placed above small paper labels that bore our names, and Mrs Rishworth went along the row scrutinising them, along with Mrs Lambert, who was about to take charge of us. There were shepherds made from bits of striped pyjama fabric; there were forerunners of the Barbie doll in six inches of tulle; there were soldiers and sailors and chefs and policemen in varying stages of dress; but there was only one black-and-white minstrel. He did rather stand out. Not just because of his colour, but also because of the standard of handiwork.

I think it was plain for all to see that this was the work of a mother. There was a tense silence while the two summer projects were judged, and then, after some conspiratorial nodding and a whispered conversation, the two adjudicators came to the front of the classroom.

The winner of the peg-doll competition is . . .' Mrs Rishworth paused for effect '. . . John Brown for his policeman.' Polite applause followed and John beamed and looked at the floor.

'And the winner of the pressed-flower competition is . . .' another pause '. . . a truly wonderful collection in two albums from Alan Titchmarsh.'

I think it was the very first time I had heard my name spoken out loud in public when it was not used as a reprimand. My name had been called out because I had won something. It had never happened before. And it had happened for something that I really had done myself.

Had mum's black-and-white-minstrel peg doll been given a prize, I would have been racked with guilt. As it was, I could hold my head up high. My plant collection had the seal of approval and I was given *The Observer's Book of Wild Animals* to prove it.

I still have it. And I still have the pressed flowers in their albums. The stamp hinges are still stuck down. And the leaves of tissue paper from the loaves of bread are still carefully in place. But there are still one or two flowers I cannot identify. That's probably because now, fifty years on, they really are 'little brown jobs'.

Grandad Hardisty and me on his allotment by the River Wharfe
in 1950. The lids of Cadbury's cocoa tins are there to frighten
off the sparrows from his sweet peas but it looks as though I
pose more of a threat.

Dad with his father, Fred, and his mother, Florrie, known to me as 'Grandma Titch'.

Mum and Uncle Bert outside 46 Ash Grove, Ilkley, in 1929. The look of the house had not changed when I was born 20 years later.

Grandma and Grandad Hardisty taking a break, and a pipe full of Condor, on the moors.

Mum and Dad with me in a
rather grand christening robe.
I must be in there somewhere.

Aged two, being held up by Mum and
watched over by Grandma Titch and
Auntie Alice.

On the beach at Blackpool
with Mum and friend in 1953.

Grandad Hardisty's terrier
Smudger showing off her sitting
position, and me showing off one
of Mum's more elaborate hand-
knits – a cardigan patterned with
two Scottie dogs.

Grandad and Grandma Hardisty with Kath, the new arrival, in the backyard of 46 Ash Grove.

Grandma Titch gets to hold the baby, too, on the back lane behind 9 Dean Street.

'The back' at the rear of 34 Nelson Road – Kath with her trike and me with my pedal car (secondhand). The flowering currant bush is in its infancy.

Smartly kitted out in turquoise shorts and a red bow tie for a walk along the prom at Morecambe with 'Uncle' John.

The Lone Ranger, aged seven, shows off his weapons in the back garden of 34 Nelson Road. Kath looks more interested in the flowers.

On the fire engine in 1955. Dad rode on it regularly, but I can only dream.

A Sunday walk down by the river. Dad's coat by Greenwoods of Ilkley; mine and Kath's and Mum's by Mrs Titchmarsh herself.

Dad's Austin A55 pickup – the first vehicle to be parked in Nelson Road.

Angelic at eleven in cassock, surplice and ruff, outside the vestry door of Ilkley parish church.

Me with Lulu, Dad with Cindy, and Kath with Wilmer in 1959. The dog lasted much longer than the rabbits.

Smartened up and kitted out for secondary school in 1960,
butter wouldn't melt . . .

What is it that makes some children more confident than others? Are they born that way? Is it nature or nurture? I've never been sure. But lack of confidence is a curse — a curse that still plagues me after fifty-odd years. I think people get irritated when you admit as much, especially if you've 'got on' and done quite well. But there is, genuinely, that feeling that sooner or later you will be found out for what you really are — an impostor; the only child in a room of adults. It's not an affectation, a display of false modesty. It is deep-seated and impossible to shift. Born, I suppose, of a lack of security. But why should it happen to someone whose childhood was loving and, for the most part, happy? And why should it still manifest itself later in life in someone whom, as far as other folk are concerned, has life sorted? I will never understand the true nature of insecurity. Perhaps those who appear confident and self-assured are just better at putting on a front than the rest of us. I wish I had the knack. Or, at least, a thicker skin.

The Dawning of Reality

I wish I could say that I had ever felt a real part of school, but I never did. Maybe it was the same for all kids, but some of them just seemed to fit in quite naturally – they were good at maths from day one, or, at the very least, seemed to have been born understanding the ground rules. I suppose the biggest mistake I made was in imagining that school would be a bit like our family. Only bigger.

It was a naïve assumption. A childish one. But then I was a child. I innocently assumed that if I was nice to everyone else, everyone else would be nice to me. It wasn't that I was a goody-goody, just that I had other things to do than look for trouble. And problems.

The fact that I had got it all wrong dawned very gradually. There was a moment, for instance, when teachers stopped calling you by your Christian name. I wondered why. Up until the age of about eight they had been happy to shout out 'Alan'. Suddenly it was 'Titchmarsh'. Sort of impersonal. And unlike 'Smith' or 'Jones', 'Titchmarsh' was such an identifiable name. There was no hiding with a name like that. No blending into the background with the Robertsons and the Taylors. Mr Rhodes had always called us by our Christian names, so why did Mr Chadwick not? Almost overnight it changed.

And Mr Chadwick never seemed to give you the benefit of the doubt. Mr Rhodes was no pushover, but he was the sort of teacher who when you said you didn't think you could do something, would encourage you to believe that you could. When you told Mr Chadwick you *could* do something, he assured you you couldn't.

I always thought I had a good sense of humour. Mum and Dad

talked about the importance of being able to 'take a joke against yourself'. I think I understood what they meant. After all, I'd never been overly serious – always trying to make people laugh, and quite happy when I succeeded. It was a kind of defence mechanism, I suppose. I didn't mind being thought silly when that was my intention. It kind of distracted folk from the fact that I hadn't really mastered long division. But one day Mr Chadwick turned all that on its head.

There was a Christmas party planned at the school. Nothing especially grand – just an afternoon off at the end of term when we would have sandwiches and buns, and play a few games. We were told that we could make a party hat out of cardboard. We were given a sheet each.

I decided that I would be a wizard and so I cut off a square of cardboard and bent it round to form a cone. What I could not do – with just two small hands – was stick it together. I asked for help. Mr Chadwick came over with the Sellotape-dispenser and stuck the two edges together while I held them in place. Then he asked me to get up. I did so. He put the now pointed hat on to my head. (I had not yet stuck on the brim, which would transform it into my wizard's hat, to be painted with stars and moons.) Then, in full view of the class, he walked me over to the corner of the room and stood me there while, in red chalk, he drew a letter 'D' in the middle of the hat.

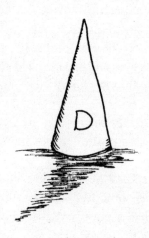

Everyone laughed. But I could not see what he was doing. I looked around me at the sniggering faces of my classmates, trying vainly to understand why it was all so funny. Only when I was told I could go and sit down again and took the hat off, did I realise what he had done.

I knew I should have laughed with the rest of them. That I should have been able to 'take a joke against myself', and yet, that afternoon, I felt betrayed. Far from being a part of the joke, I was the butt of it because I could not see what he was doing.

It was a simple, silly thing. The sort of thing that a teacher would do without a moment's thought, and yet it has lived with me all these years and I have never forgotten that moment of what to me – in the middle of what should have been a jolly, carefree afternoon – was one of the most shaming and upsetting moments of my life. Had I regarded myself as in any way bright, it would not have mattered. It would have been an obvious joke. But the grain of truth that it contained – that I was, indeed, a dunce – wounded me to the heart.

You could argue that I should have been more thick-skinned, less sensitive. But the fact remains that on that day I felt more isolated, more alone, more marginalised than I had ever felt before. And all because of a silly hat.

Dad's limited record collection wasn't the most comprehensive intro-
duction to music. The red leatherette-covered Fidelity gramophone,
bought from Mrs Woodrup's catalogue, could at least play an LP with
the lid closed, which pleased my mother's tidy nature, but the collection
of discs was slow in building up. There was an Ace of Clubs LP of
Mendelssohn's 'Fingal's Cave', the Band of the Royal Marines
playing military marches, an EP of Maria Callas singing the 'Easter
Hymn' from Cavalleria Rusticana and, my own contribution, –
Russ Conway playing 'China Tea'.

Nevertheless, Dad had loved music and singing from an early age,
and when he came home one evening with another EP of Mario Lanza
giving vent to the 'Drinking Song' from The Student Prince, his
collection was almost complete. Had he been able to find a recording of
Richard Tauber singing 'You Are My Heart's Delight', his cup would
have overflowed. To make up for this deficiency, he would sing it to my
mother instead.

It didn't put me off.

The Voice

T he inference was that it wasn't very good. 'It's a bit reedy,' said bandy-legged Mr Atkinson, the choir master, when he heard me speak. Then he sat down at the piano in the vestry and played a few arpeggios. 'Right. Sing these notes.' He launched into his first scale. There was no 'How nice to see you'. 'How good of you to come' or 'So you want to be a choirboy?' Just 'Sing these notes'.

He seemed surprised when I could, and when I managed to reach 'E' above top 'C'. He looked over the top of his thick horn-rimmed glasses, and I saw that his eyebrows were black and bushy like hairy caterpillars. From the waistcoat of his grey suit hung a delicate gold watch chain. He took out the timepiece and looked at it. 'Right. You can start on Monday.' Why he needed the watch to work out what day I was to start I couldn't understand, but I do remember being relieved.

My acceptance into the ranks of All Saints Parish Church Choir must also have been a relief to my dad, who had been a member since he, too, had been a lad. The high spot had been when he sang at the Albert Hall. Not on his own, he was at pains to point out, but as part of the choir at some big festival. I, in my usual way, accepted that my future Sundays were mapped out. But then I did enjoy singing. It gave me a kind of freedom, in my head, if not in terms of where I could go on Sundays.

I discovered I could sing at junior school. Mrs Rishworth, chatelaine of the second form, was the musical one, forever putting together some small percussion orchestra or choir. With tiny drums, cymbals, triangles, tambourines and 'clappers' (she thought 'casta-nets' too exotic a word for our juvenile northern vocabularies), we would bang away in time to either her conducting or the flailing arm of another pupil she thought had promise. It was usually a girl called Dale Bryce, who had about as much style as a metronome. Her face would remain totally expressionless, and she would repeatedly draw in the air a perfect triangle, as one might with a sparkler on Bonfire Night; but there was no passion, no liberties with the rhythm. There she stood with her neat brown hair pulled back into a ponytail, her stout frame encased in a grey woollen jumper and pleated skirt, evincing not a grain of emotion and staring straight ahead as her arm quartered the air.

How I longed to get hold of that stick. I had just watched Sir Malcolm Sargent on *Last Night of the Proms* and knew exactly what conducting was about. You had to feel the music, transmit its emotion. (What you also had to be able to do was read it, but that seemed relatively unimportant. The main thing was enthusiasm.)

Then one day Mrs Rishworth gave in to my pleadings (probably in the interests of a quiet life) and let me have a go. I took the baton – a wooden drumstick – and approached the podium, a large atlas. Magisterially I lifted up my arms and checked, with raised eyebrows, that I had their attention. Then I brought my arms down and began conducting with all the passion of a maestro, remembering to close my eyes part of the time, the better to concentrate.

My moment of glory did not last long. I think it was about five bars.

'No, no, no!' Mrs Rishworth wailed. 'That won't do at all.' The drumstick was wrested from my grasp and I was sent back to my clappers, saddened that such an injustice could be allowed, that plodding beats were somehow preferable to heart and soul. It was a long walk, from the atlas to the back row of the clapper department. I tried not to look to right or left. Tried to ignore the sniggers. John Brown passed me my little black instrument – three pieces of wood held together by a shoelace – but he didn't meet my eye.

Dale Bryce took up the drumstick once more and I noticed that this time her inscrutable expression bore the faintest hint of a smug smile. I did my best to make my clappers keep time, but my heart was no longer in it.

I don't know that I particularly wanted to become a choirboy, in the same way that I don't know if I was religious. I know that I believed in God, because my mum and dad did and if I was theirs, then I must, too.

Not that they ever talked about it. It was just what you did. Like eating. And we never said grace before meals. Mum thought that people who did that were showing off. Far too ostentatious. Public demonstrations of faith were confined to church, and low church at that. Mum became very uneasy one Sunday when, to demonstrate some point or other, the vicar lit a candle. From my seat in the choir stalls I could see her bridling in the pews, clenching her hands in her lap and raising her shoulders. Her relief when he blew it out at the end of the demonstration was palpable. Quite what she would have made of the 'peace' I can't imagine. She'd have probably become an agnostic.

But I was taught to say my prayers at night before I went to sleep. In summer I knealed by the bed, but in winter, when it was cold, and the ice patterns crept up the inside of the windowpane, I was allowed to say them in bed. They were always the same: 'Gentle Jesus, meek and mild, look upon a little child; pity my simplicity, give me grace to come to thee. Amen.' Then there would be the 'God-blesses' – encompassing the immediate family, as far as grandparents, and pets.

I attended Sunday school before I joined the choir. It was rather a desultory affair. There were only eight of us; a mixture of children from devout families and from families whose parents just wanted a bit of peace and quiet on a Sunday afternoon. My own parents were a cross between the two. We were taken to the hall of the junior school by the vicar's wife – Mrs Cook – a squat lady with bad teeth and grey hair drawn up into a bun from which it always seemed to be escaping in unruly wisps. She would bang out a hymn on the piano at the beginning, then explain a parable – the lost sheep or the sower – and then bang out another hymn at the end. Only half a dozen of them were deemed appropriate – 'All things bright and beautiful' and 'Glad that I live am I, that the sky is blue' were favourites. There might be a bit of crayoning in a book. Then our motley little band would be shepherded up the road and handed back to our parents. I don't remember being anything other than bored.

At least at choir there were other lads, and we did have a bit of a laugh, especially on Mondays, which were 'boys only' rehearsals. There must have been about a dozen of us. None of us were what you might call 'holy'. A few of us did enjoy singing, but the rest were there for the money. Sixpence a week, I think, with a shilling extra for a wedding. We were paid four times a year and in spite of patchy attendance, everybody turned up for rehearsal on pay day.

We wore purple cassocks and white surplices and ruffs. They were freshly laundered only for Easter and Christmas, and between the two festivals they became progressively greyer until once more the Lakeland Laundry down Leeds Road worked its washday magic.

The difficulty for me was finding a cassock that was short enough. At four feet nothing, I was swamped by most of them, and if I wasn't in first on a Sunday morning, I would end up mounting the chancel steps with a train that would not have disgraced the Queen at her coronation. The surplice, too, could be so all-enveloping that I would have difficulty in locating my arms, come the first hymn.

The ruffs we hated. When they were freshly starched and laundered, they would cut into your neck like a knife, especially if you got one that was too tight. The finishing touch was provided by a medal that dangled round our necks. We'd done nothing to earn them. They were oval and bronze and bore the crest of the Royal School of Church Music, which gave us an air of legitimacy. The two head boys had medals with red ribbon, we lower mortals made do with pale-blue, and the week after week of Trinity, when services seemed to slip into a sort of unremarkable plod, were made up for by the feast days like Easter and Whitsuntide, Palm Sunday and Christmas, when we'd process round the outside of the church and walk in through the Norman arch of the south door, singing a stirring hymn – 'Jesus Christ is risen today, alleluia!' or 'O come, all ye faithful'. At the sight of our white surplices billowing in the wind, the traffic would slow on Leeds Road and Church Street to watch our progress, and we felt ridiculously important, and very holy. Even Peter Earle, his red hair smarmed down for the occasion, could manage to look angelic. Passers-by wouldn't be able to see the catapult in his right pocket and the bubblegum in his left.

In the boring bits – the twenty-five-minute sermon from our long-winded Welsh curate, or the intercessions – we'd chew bubblegum and read the latest *War Picture Library* with black-and-white illustrations of World War II battles. As the curate spoke of Pharisees and gentiles, we were in the thrall of German commandants who said, 'Achtung, pig-dog!' and 'Gott in Himmel, vas is going on?' until we heard the magic words 'And so to God the Father, God the Son and God the Holy Ghost, be ascribed all that is most justly due . . .' at which point we would scrabble to put away

the magazines, take out the bubblegum and stick it under the book rest of the pew and shuffle the pages of our hymn books to the right place. When we stood up to sing 'Jesu, good above all other', the congregation would never have guessed that we weren't.

On Thursdays we rehearsed with the men – Dad and Harry Chambers were tenors at around five foot six inches tall; Uncle George Pennock, my godfather, was six foot something, and a bass, so I always assumed that the depth of your voice had something to do with your height. I am now five feet eight and a half and a tenor. I have no reason to disbelieve my earlier theory.

The presence of the men meant that we had to behave. If we

didn't, we got clouted. Peter Earle's ear was usually as red as his hair due to Harry Chambers clouting it with his hymn book for some perceived misdemeanour. 'Aw, gerroff! I'll tell my dad!' was Peter's usual pathetic threat. He never did. He knew he'd get another clout from his dad.

So if we let off steam, it was on Mondays. That was when Mr Atkinson was on his own. He had little control at the best of times, and the nearest he came to raising his voice was to say, 'Boys, boys!' in his rather quavering voice when our high spirits threatened to bring proceedings to a halt.

His conducting, though marginally more exciting than that of Dale Bryce, was not exactly of symphonic standard, and his vocal coaching was confined to the warning 'Don't force it!' – an exhortation that caused great glee when directed at David Fawcett, who stood next to me. It was fully ten minutes before Mr Atkinson regained control after issuing the instruction 'Don't force it, Fawcett.' But then we were easily distracted.

When Mr Atkinson was not there, then the organist, Arthur Pickett, had to master both his instrument and crowd control, and the maintenance of discipline was, if anything, even more shaky. Arthur was a lovely man, but he had a stammer.

'We're going to sing tha, tha, tha f-f-f-f-first hymn on tha, tha, tha sheet I've just ga-ga-ga-given out . . .'

It was a disability of which the humour was exploited to the full by Peter Earle, who would stand behind him during a particularly sterterous passage and mime the words to the rest of us. We didn't want to laugh. We knew we were being unkind. And yet it was impossible not to be buoyed along by Peter's ridiculous impersonation.

Eventually Arthur would cotton on to the situation and lose his temper; turning round, catching hold of Peter's ear and propelling him into the pew in front of him with practised ease.

On summer evenings, after choir practice, we'd wander round the churchyard before we went home, wading through the long grass, discharging clouds of pollen into the still, warm air and conjuring up stories under the conker trees about who was buried where. With a morbid curiosity we'd look for the graves of babies and infants who had died when they were younger than we were, and try to find the oldest inhabitant – a posh lady from Middleton who'd lived into her nineties.

One grave had above it a sort of raised triangular tomb, a bit like a house roof, with a stone cross embossed on it. It stood in a particularly shady part of the graveyard out of sight of the vestry door. The air there was always cold, whatever the time of year. Peter Earle said it was because it was the devil's grave.

So it was, that whenever a new choirboy was installed, he was initiated on the devil's grave. We'd warn him of the impending ceremony and take delight in his widening eyes. For several weeks he would be notified of the moment when, after a chosen choir practice, he would be taken to the devil's grave and held down on it while terrible things were done to him.

The threat was everything. When the moment arrived, he'd be taken by the arms, kicking and screaming. Someone would bind a hanky round his mouth to gag him. It would probably not be a clean one. It would be tied in a tight knot at the back, and then he'd be hauled across the graveyard, and as the kicking and struggling reached its height, he'd be held down on his back, with the cross of the devil's grave digging into his spine as the rest of us tickled him. The cries of fear and agony would give way to helpless laughter, and then the gag would be removed and the victim would vent his spleen – 'Rotten buggers!' – expletives that were the result of relief as much as anger.

Then, at the sight of Mr Atkinson coming out of the vestry with his overcoat on, his music case tucked under his arm and his majestic grey trilby in place, we'd run off home, laughing that we'd been able to con yet another unsuspecting choirboy into thinking that a fate worse than death was waiting for him on the devil's grave.

By way of a sop, more than anything else, we were taken on a choir trip once a year in summer. It would always be to the same place – Morecambe, where it usually rained – with lunch in the Winter Gardens and a trip to the menagerie at Heysham Head as the high spot. There was nothing much there – just a few flea-bitten monkeys and some slot machines and seedy shops that sold cheap souvenirs. You could guarantee that Peter Earle would manage to find something that would astonish the rest of us. One year it was a Biro that you could tilt so that a girl in a swimsuit became naked before your very eyes. Apart from seeing my mother breastfeeding my sister when I was five, it was my very first glimpse of tits; I remember feeling rather excited. It was almost confiscated by Arthur Pickett, but somehow Peter Earle managed to get round him and he let him off, so that we all tumbled happily off the train back at Ilkley in the late evening, smelling of chips and wet gaberdine, and hiding any evidence of schoolboy lasciviousness.

These were times of happiness and uneventfulness in the main. Church attendance at matins and evensong on a Sunday brought a kind of calming routine to the end of the week. Though we were always told that Sunday was the first day of the week, it seemed more like a sedate finale. Despite often being possessed of a kind of dull unpredictability, it did make the prospect of school on Monday seem less daunting. At least there something would happen, and you wouldn't have to go home after church and play quietly while your parents slept in their easy chairs after lunch, waiting for the moment when you could go out for a walk on the moors or by the river and actually make use of the day off.

There were, in spite of the routine monotony of it all, a handful of memorable days in church: the day Arthur Pickett got married and we sang for him. We were all stunned that the lady who said yes was actually quite dishy; somehow we'd never seen him as the marrying type – he was married to the church organ, and the glass factory he ran during the week. To our surprise, and maybe even disappointment, he managed to get through the service with hardly a stammer – even in the vows.

The saddest day of all came when we sang at the funeral of Mr Atkinson's wife. She had come to choir practices occasionally and played the organ for her husband when Arthur Pickett was away. She was quietly spoken and well dressed – the precise female equivalent of her husband. She usually wore a hat. I can see her at the organ, dressed in peach silk, serenely playing some tricky passage while her husband coached the handful of average junior-school children in an attempt to turn them into something worth hearing of a Sunday.

Their two grandsons – David and Jonathan – proved by their names alone that this was a family of some piety, though as head boys of the choir (by virtue of their height as much as nepotism – they would have looked ridiculous in rank and file), they could be every bit as mischievous as the rest of us.

The news of her death was told to us in hushed tones by one of the men – I can't remember which. But we all left choir practice feeling saddened and slightly ashamed that we had not been nicer to Mr Atkinson. He never came back.

We discovered later the true tragedy of the situation. Mrs Atkinson had collapsed in the drive of their house in Menston. Mr Atkinson had not seen her go down. He'd been backing the car out of the garage. As a result, he drove the car over her body. She would most likely have been dead already, they said, but it did not take much imagination to understand how he must have felt.

There was a poignancy to choir practices after that. Peter Earle was well behaved; unwilling to cause a fuss even in Arthur Pickett's most hesitant speeches.

Mrs Atkinson should have passed away quietly and without drama. She was a gentle lady. She had a gentle husband. They both went to church on a Sunday. Somehow it didn't seem fair. But at least she was old. Old people died regularly; young people did not. At least, not usually.

My dad worked for a plumber called Billy Lawson. He was older than Dad; a quiet, self-contained sort of man with a flat cap and a hooked nose. He lived on the edge of town with his sister, Maggie, and their niece, Kathleen. I am not sure what happened to Kathleen's parents, or whether Billy and Maggie had officially adopted her. In any event, they treated her as their own child, and as they were a good deal older than most parents and a good deal better off, they spoiled her rotten.

It didn't seem to affect her. She was a nice girl – friendly, if a bit quiet – and Maggie seemed keen that Kathleen and I should be friends. We did not see a lot of each other, but I remember vividly a visit to Bradford Alhambra on her birthday, when Charlie Cairoli, the clown, wished her a happy birthday from the stage halfway through the performance. I was hugely impressed, and Kathleen wore a pink mohair cardigan and looked suitably embarrassed.

My mother did not encourage the friendship. Whether it was because she didn't want me making friends with the boss's daughter or because Kathleen was a Catholic I don't know. Mum was not a religious fanatic; she would have argued that she was not at all prejudiced against other religions. She just thought that people who were C. of E. didn't marry Catholics – simple as that – so as far as she was concerned, it was better if potential relationships were nipped in the bud before things became too complicated.

I can't have been overly concerned. I didn't see Kathleen again until we were in our early teens. Then I caught sight of her sitting in the passenger seat of Billy Lawson's car when I went to meet my dad from work. My dad was inside talking to her dad, and she was waiting patiently to be driven home.

I could hardly believe my eyes. She was stunning. The tiny little girl in the pink cardigan was now a shapely young woman with a crisp white blouse and olive skin – her dark-brown eyes flashing in the afternoon sun.

'Hello, Alan,' she said softly. 'How are you?'

My legs turned to jelly and I tried to stop my mouth from falling open. I failed.

Kathleen laughed gently. 'Remember me?'

I nodded. 'At the theatre.'

'Yes,' she said. 'How are you?' She got out of the car and leaned against the roof, and in those few moments I fell in love. At least, I thought I did. It wasn't just that she was stunningly attractive; there was a warmth about her, a sort of serenity.

A few minutes later Billy came out. He nodded at me and murmured a greeting – as always, polite and, as always, softly spoken. Kathleen said goodbye, adding that it was nice to see me again, and slid back into the car. She turned round and waved as Billy Lawson's Austin Cambridge slid out of sight round the corner, and I saw, again, the flash of those dark-brown eyes and the knowing smile.

Back home, I considered asking my dad what I should do. But I thought the better of it. I mean, what could he do? Tell Billy that I fancied her and ask him if she could come on a date? No. I'd have to sort it out myself. And I wouldn't say anything to Mum. She'd be against it, anyway, for reasons already discussed. And so I brooded and did nothing. But the look on Kathleen's face I could not get out of my mind. It had a warmth I had never seen before, and her eyes seemed to see into my soul. A month later Kathleen Lawson died of leukaemia.

I never said anything to my mum or my dad about our meeting. I didn't need anybody to know what had happened between us. Apparently Kathleen had been ill for some time. They knew she was going to die. And so did she. I climbed up to my attic room and stared out of the window towards the purple moors. Below me, the rest of the curtains in the street were closed. I closed the curtains on my own window, and sat on the bed until long after it was dark.

Running at right angles to the top of Brook Street is the Grove. This is Ilkley's smartest street. Select. It has a Betty's café and is lined with flowering cherry trees that are awash with pink blossom in spring. There are moments in April when Ilkley looks like Harrogate. But only moments. Ilkley residents regard Harrogate as pretentious. A town with ideas above its station. Talk to them in Harrogate about Ilkley and they'll smile sympathetically and move the conversation on.

The Grove used to have the art-deco-inspired Bluebird Café – all chrome and dark-blue Vitrolite – where Grandma Titch worked as a 'nippy' with 'silver service and six plates up each arm' until she was seventy-six and my dad suggested she might ease up a little. She cut the plates down to five.

Mr Guy, the hairdresser, operates in a basement at the far end of the Grove on the opposite side to where the Bluebird used to be. It's where my mum used to have her hair done, the same place as the now dowager Duchess of Devonshire, when she was up at Bolton Abbey. Mum rather liked that.

She didn't know the Duchess of Devonshire, but the Duchess knows me, and knew that my mother used the same hairdresser.

My mother died four years ago now. She was crippled with arthritis at the end, but her hearing was always sharp as a razor. One day Mr Guy bent over her in the chair and said, 'The Duchess of Devonshire was enquiring after you, Mrs Titchmarsh.'

My mother looked round the salon and noticed that one or two of the ladies were under driers. 'I'm sorry?' she asked.

'THE DUCHESS OF DEVONSHIRE WAS ENQUIR-ING AFTER YOU!'

'Oh, was she? That's nice of her.'

The Posh End

I t wasn't an inferiority complex – just a realistic assessment of our social differences. The folk who lived 'up the Grove' were different from us, though, as Grandad Hardisty put it, the difference was that 'They owed more money.'

Every now and again I'd find myself in the company of someone from the select end of town. My cousin David took me there once. We didn't socialise as a rule; David was a year or so older than me and that meant different classes at school and a different set of friends. But for some reason or other we'd found ourselves in each other's company on one particular day and he took me to meet Tim. There were instructions on the way. 'Just remember, you've got to talk posh,' he instructed.

I'd never practised. I was stuck with 'bath' and 'grass' and felt odd saying 'barth' and 'grarss'. It did occur to me that unless the conversation got round to personal hygiene, it would be unlikely that I should have to worry about the first word, but if we played football on his lawn, I could be in trouble.

'What are we going to do?' I asked.

'Just muck around.'

'Do they muck around up there?'

'Course. They're just like us. Only posher.'

I was not convinced. It sounded to me like a recipe for disaster. If Tim was a friend of David's, did he think David was posh, too? Had David put on his posh accent whenever he was in Tim's company?

I tried to find excuses not to go, but it was no use. I had nothing else to do except tag along.

'And when he asks what your dad does, say he's in management,' said David.

'He's a plumber.'

'Well, he can still manage, can't he?'

I began to feel a bit queasy. We walked up towards the smart end of town, under the umbrellas of pink cherry blossom on the Grove that were shedding their petals like confetti, and then past the shops into the residential area. The Grove becomes Grove Road at its far end and leads upwards and westwards out of the town to a series of smarter streets with stone-built houses, some with little turrets and touches of Victorian Gothic or mock Tudor in King's Road and Victoria Road; even the names have a regal ring to them.

Nelson Road, where I lived, was east of the town. The houses here were two up, two down with an attic and a cellar, and their stonework was blackened by a century of soot. Along with Wellington Road, Trafalgar Road and Nile Road, Nelson Road was named after heroes who would presumably inspire the workers to achieve greater things. There was also Brewery Road, which would offer comfort when all else failed.

David himself did live up the smarter end – just off Queen's Road. This was because Auntie Jenny cleaned for a large house up there and they had a tied cottage – Shandon Cottage – which always smelled of damp. Clearly he got to meet a better class of person than I did down the east end of town.

'Come on, don't dawdle.'

'I'm not dawdling.' But I was. I walked as slowly as I could, hoping, perhaps, that Tim might be a stickler for punctuality and that if we were late he would have gone out.

We reached a smart wrought-iron gate – a double one – across a wide tarmac drive. David opened it and strode purposefully up to the front door. They had a bell. And a drive. And double gates. He rang the bell. I shifted my weight from one foot to the other.

The door was opened by a fresh-faced youth with thick, dark hair.

'Helleao,' said David.

'Hi,' said Tim.

David turned to introduce me. 'This is Ellan.'

I smiled as bravely as I could and said, 'Hi!' It seemed a safer bet than, 'Helleao.'

'Come in,' said Tim, holding the door open and stepping back into the house.

We crossed the threshold – David eagerly, myself reluctantly – and I spent the next two minutes wiping my feet on the doormat.

The conversation was stilted. It wasn't that Tim was unfriendly, but that David seemed keen to steer the conversation where it did not naturally want to go.

'Ellan's very keen on gardening,' he volunteered.

It was not the most natural of conversational gambits for ten-year-olds. Even those who lived up the Grove.

'Really?' Tim looked sympathetic. 'Would you like to come and look at the rose garden?'

I nodded.

We were taken through the house, which had very deep-fitted carpets into which my shoes sank. I fought to keep my balance. Then we were led through a chintzy sitting room, awash with shiny mahogany furniture dotted with silver, and out through the French windows into a formal rose garden.

Tim, anxious to please, asked, 'Would you like to do some gardening?'

I thought this was a daft idea. And anyway, the rose garden was immaculate with its formal beds and dusty grey earth. They clearly had a gardener and I couldn't see him being best pleased if the son of the household got a couple of mates round to tackle his sacred rose beds.

'No . . . really . . . it's fine,' I offered.

'No problem. The shed's over here.'

He led the way across the immaculately striped lawn that bordered the rose garden, and guided us to a stone outbuilding with stable doors. He swung on the sneck and opened both doors to reveal an armoury of shiny tools hanging on the whitewashed walls.

'Which ones will be best?'

I was out of my depth. 'No . . . I think we should just look . . .'

David dug me in the ribs and shot me a look of irritation.

'Will these do?' asked Tim.

He pulled down a rake, a Dutch hoe and a fork.

'I suppose . . .' was the best I could do.

And so, armed with a tool apiece, we followed Tim across the hallowed turf and began to prod at the grey dust underneath the rose bushes. Tim had the fork, which he pushed into the ground and wiggled about a bit. He had clearly never used it before. David set to raking the level earth even leveller, and I hoed, scrutinising the soil for the merest suggestion of a weed.

David said, 'Ellan loves doing this, don't you, Ellan?'

The best I could manage was a weak smile. Tim looked at me pityingly. We had not been forking, raking and hoeing for more than a couple of minutes when a woman's voice rang out across the garden.

'Timothy! What *are* you doing?'

'A bit of gardening, Mum. Alan's a keen gardener.'

The lady in the smart yellow suit, with pearls at her throat, who was standing at the open French windows looked pained. 'Really? Well, Burgess only did the rose beds yesterday and he won't be very happy if you make a mess of them.' The neatly raked earth steadfastly refused to swallow me up.

Tim looked at us apologetically and took from us the rake and the hoe. 'How about an ice cream?'

'Leovely,' said David.

I said nothing, but followed the two of them – first back to the shed to replace the tools (I worried that we hadn't polished them), then to the back door of the house. We followed Tim to a small utility room. Along one wall was a large white box with an enormous lid. It must have been six feet long, four feet high and three feet deep. He lifted the lid and revealed box after box of ice creams and lollies. We had an icebox in our new fridge, but it was only six inches square. In it, my mum could make half a dozen iced lollies with wooden sticks in a sort of aluminium mould. She poured orange squash into the holes and in a few hours my sister and I could have a lolly that lost its flavour and its colour and its stick after just two minutes of sucking.

In Tim's freezer, there were choc ices and strawberry mivvies, tubs of soft ice cream and lollies of all flavours – raspberry, strawberry, lemon and lime, and orange.

'What would you like?' he asked.

David asked for a strawberry mivvi; I said that an orange lolly would be fine.

We got what we asked for, and then Tim said he was really sorry but he had to go now and be somewhere else. It was the best thing I'd heard all day, but I tried to look disappointed.

We walked round the side of the house now, rather than through it, which came as a great relief. I was terrified of dripping on the carpet.

'*Au revoir*, Tim,' offered David.

'Bye,' was the best I could do, as we walked down the drive sucking our lollies. David looked pleased with himself and was wiping the pink juice from his chin.

'Great i'n't it? Bein' posh?'

I didn't say anything. I just kept on sucking my lolly. It was big and full of flavour, but somehow it wasn't nearly as much fun as the ones Mum made in her little icebox back home.

Not all encounters with the folk up the posh end were quite so excruciating. It wasn't long before I learned that the really well-to-do were usually people who had the same manners as we had and who were kind and considerate whatever your background. And they didn't seem to mind if you said 'bath' and 'grass'.

The Brooksbanks lived in the largest house in Grove Road. It was right at the top and invisible from the entrance gates, which led on to a large drive that swirled downhill in a generous arc. Their chauffeur, Victor Bean, was a bellringer with Mum and Dad, and spoke of his employers in hushed tones and with the utmost respect. They called him 'Bean' and he called them 'sir' and 'madam'. Victor wore a uniform and a peaked cap when he was at work, and drove Mr Brooksbank into Bradford every morning in a very large and shiny car. I think Mr Brooksbank was in wool.

Mr and Mrs Brooksbank were both churchgoers, and both had a

regal bearing – he was tall with wisps of white hair combed across his broad brow. He always wore pale-grey suits. Mrs Brooksbank wore floral-print dresses and sometimes a fur wrap. She was an ample woman for whom the word 'largesse' could have been invented.

Every year, on the night before Christmas Eve, the boys of the church choir would wend their way up Grove Road, knocking on the door of selected houses and singing carols. At the end of the evening, charitable donations not having been invented back then, the proceeds were divided between us as a sort of Christmas bonus.

The last house, at around half past eight, would always be the Brooksbanks'. They would be waiting for us with orange squash and biscuits.

Huddled together against the bitter cold that whipped down off the moors, we'd pick our way down the curving drive that would have been swept clear of snow. The amber glow of lights would be obscured at first by the welter of laurel and holly that offered the large Victorian mansion total privacy against prying eyes. Eventually the enormous archway of the front door would heave into view, its wrought-iron lantern now clearly visible, and Arthur Pickett would ring the bell as we all stamped our feet to keep warm.

There would be eight or ten of us, usually – enough to make a decent stab at 'The holly and the ivy' and 'Away in a manger' even if, by this stage, we had begun to feel a bit hoarse.

The door would be opened by the butler, and we'd be ushered into the hallway. Tim's hall had nothing on this one. It was huge, with a wide staircase and galleried landing that looked like something out of *My Fair Lady*. All the way up were paintings of hunting scenes and portraits of important-looking people in elaborate costumes. As scenes go, it was tremendously impressive, and yet, for some reason, not the slightest bit intimidating.

Across the hallway, the polished wood double doors that led to the drawing room would be open, and a fire would be lit in the massive grate with its moulded surround. In a corner stood a grand piano, covered with photographs in silver frames.

Mr and Mrs Brooksbank would walk forward from the fire and greet us as though we were long-lost relatives. 'So nice to see you again. Thank you so much for coming. You must be frozen. Do warm yourselves by the fire before you start.'

These were the sort of folk from 'up the Grove' for whom my parents had the utmost respect. They were not 'snooty' like some folk from that end of town; they were polite when they came into Uncle Bert's grocer's shop, and had good manners, just like Mum and Uncle Bert. They treated their staff well and paid their plumbing and grocery bills on time and in full. They were, in short, 'nice people'.

We took off our coats and soon felt the benefit of the crackling fire before Arthur sat at the piano and we launched into 'Once in Royal' and 'The Angel Gabriel from heaven came', eyeing up the bourbon biscuits, custard creams and orange squash that stood on the gleaming mahogany side table in readiness for our finale. That was always 'Hark! the herald angels sing', and the prospect of squash and biscuits always gave us additional energy for our very last carol before Christmas Day.

There would be glowing faces from us, and hearty thank yous from the Brooksbanks and their daughter, who appeared every Christmas wearing a long tartan skirt that somehow added to the festive feel.

'Do come and have some refreshments,' Mrs Brooksbank urged. She reminded me of the Queen Mother, both in appearance and manner, and all of us felt pleased that she wanted us to be in her house at Christmas, sharing her hospitality. There was never the faintest suspicion of 'them and us' about it. We were all there to celebrate Christmas and to enjoy being in the grand house with the sound of carols ringing around the rafters.

Just as David had informed Tim of my interest in gardening, someone took it into their heads to inform Mrs Brooksbank of my interest in art. It was exactly that – an interest. I was neither especially well informed nor particularly accomplished, but I was interested and loved looking at paintings. Perhaps she would think that I knew more than I did. The warning bells began to ring. But I needn't have worried.

'How very nice,' she said. 'Would you like to see some paintings?'

Instead of a mute and embarrassed nod, I plucked up my courage and replied that yes, I would love to, and so, while the others tucked into the bourbons and the custard creams, I was led out of the drawing room by Mrs Brooksbank and into the hall.

'Come with me,' she instructed, climbing the wide staircase with its patterned Indian carpet until we reached the galleried landing. Here, with the sparkling chandelier at eye level, and above the waist-high dark oak panelling, hung landscapes and portraits of varying age. There were some men in wigs and frock coats, others of ladies in velvet gowns, the folds beautifully painted. There were landscapes of Yorkshire and Scotland, of streams and rivers, woodland and moorland. It was as impressive as Leeds City Art Gallery to my young and untutored eyes, and she and I had it all to ourselves.

I listened as she told me about the different paintings – about Peter Lely and Godfrey Kneller, Joseph Farquharson and Atkinson Grimshaw, but whether these were the artists whose works I was looking at I cannot say – I was lost in a maze of wonder among the folds of velvet and the dense forests.

'So which one do you like best?' she asked at the end of our circuit of the landing.

I did not have to think for long. There was a portrait of a young man, perhaps ten years older than I was, holding a gun at his waist and gazing out over the landscape behind him. He wore a pale-blue shirt and dark trousers, and had a faraway look in his eye. His lips were half smiling; he seemed comfortable and at ease with himself.

'That one,' I replied, without hesitation.

'Ah,' said Mrs Brooksbank. There was a note of wistfulness in her voice. 'That's my son.'

'Oh.'

'Yes. I'm not sure about the likeness, but I always said that I would know that it was my son by his hands.'

I felt that it was a sad thing to say, and as I looked at her I could see that her eyes were filled with tears. She had left me now and was with him for a few moments. Up on that patch of Yorkshire moorland over which he was gazing. Downstairs, her husband and daughter were entertaining the choirboys for Christmas. There was no sign of her son. I did not like to ask if he had died, or why he was not with her at Christmas. It didn't seem the right time.

I stood still and waited. Mrs Brooksbank reached out and ran her finger down the boy's hand. 'Perfect hands.' Then she cleared her throat and said, 'Shall we go down now? You must be very thirsty.'

From the moors, the centre of town is clearly visible. There are several churches: the tall spire of 'The Congs' – the Congregational church – lately renamed Christ Church, and the dumpy Norman tower of All Saints where I sang as a choirboy. I can see the outdoor swimming pool where I swam my first length and earned a clockwork tugboat, the station from which the trains took us to Leeds to shop and, in the other direction, to Morecambe on choir trips, the rugby club where I had my twenty-first birthday party (the only time I've ever been there) and cricket fields and football fields on the other side of the river.

The view from the Cow and Calf changes as you look beyond the town to the east. Ben Rhydding is the name given to the residential area that was built at the time when spas were at the height of their popularity – the name invented for its bucolic ring. I suppose Ben Rhydding sounds to strangers like the lower slopes of a Scottish mountain, simply reeking of heather and bilberries and drenched in health-giving air.

Directly opposite, on the North side of the valley, are Middleton Woods – among the finest bluebell woods in Britain and a place where a young lad with an interest in nature can find all kinds of birds and wild flowers, small mammals and fungi.

Back to Nature

M um said she thought Peter Scott looked like a duck. It wasn't meant to be an unkind remark. It was his furrowed brow she meant, rather than his lack of height. There was a picture of a mallard in one of my nature books and once she'd made the comparison I found it hard to ignore. Many years later I met Sir Peter Scott at Slimbridge when he launched a fund-raising appeal called 'Doodle-a-duck'. I hadn't the nerve to tell him.

The urge to be out with wildlife was fostered from the moment we got the television. It was not one of those bulky pieces of furniture, the size of a radiogram, with a small screen in the top. Our neat cabinet stood on a table in the corner of the front room. It was a Pye, with a sloping front and two knobs – one for volume, the other for brightness. Somewhere round the back, there was a 'horizontal hold' and a 'vertical hold', which always sounded to me like wrestling moves. Dad would fiddle with one of them when the picture started to slip from side to side or up and down. The tuner was another knob on the side of the mahogany casing, but as we only had one BBC channel for a few years after we got it, the knob was seldom twiddled.

The programmes I watched were all to do with nature. Apart from *Out of Doors*, I was allowed to stay up for Peter Scott's *Look* and for *On Safari* with Armand and Michaela Denis. The Denises were a strange couple, clearly foreign. They both wore safari suits, which I assumed you had to do when roaming around anywhere warmer than Yorkshire. She had blonde hair and appeared younger than him. Armand had a toothbrush moustache and horn-rimmed glasses, and his voice sounded as though he was speaking through a kazoo. I remember them riding a rhinoceros and speaking very earnestly about the experience.

Any programme to do with the sea was presented either by Jacques Cousteau or by another husband and wife team, Hans and Lotte Hass. I began to get used to naturalists with strong foreign accents, though coupled with the sound of bubbles from their diving equipment, Hans and Lotte's commentary was not always easy to understand.

I was on safer ground with the more youthful, and English, David Attenborough, whose *Zoo Quest* seemed to take him all over the globe in search of rare animals that could be brought back to Regent's Park or Whipsnade.

David had a safari suit, too, but his did not look nearly so ridiculous as that of Armand Denis. He was young and dashing – a great role model for any aspiring naturalist – and the hushed and confidential tones he used even then seemed directed especially at me, as he revealed some secret about the three-toed sloth, or tried to avoid being strangled by chimpanzees.

I moved on to David, intellectually speaking, from Johnny Morris, whose home patch was Bristol Zoo. Johnny would give the animals he was commenting on funny voices. They were always appropriate, and at first I wondered why David Attenborough didn't do the same. Perhaps he couldn't do voices.

It didn't matter. I was hooked on these programmes, along with *Gardening Club* on a Friday night, when Percy Thrower, in a three-piece suit and tie, would wander through the studio garden into the greenhouse that clearly had no glass. Here, he would take off his jacket, hang it on a hook behind the door, roll up his sleeves and get stuck into a bit of potting or pricking out on the bench.

Once the credits of these programmes rolled, I would be up and out of the house, pretending to be either a naturalist or a gardener, depending on the programme's content. Hans and Lottie Hass were hard to emulate, but David and Johnny were easier. Peter Scott was way too clever for me to even approach.

Sometimes, in *Children's Hour*, George Cansdale would be brought in to talk about snakes or bushbabies. Cansdale looked like a bank manager in a grey suit, and he had iron-grey hair and the same sort of toothbrush moustache as Armand Denis.

On one occasion he came to talk to the Wharfedale Naturalists' Society and I sat in the front row, eager to see in real life a man whom I had only ever glimpsed on the television. He was taller, and the suit and hair even greyer, but he did bring his snakes with him. They were in cloth drawstring bags, just like the bag I took to school with my pumps in.

Cansdale pulled out the snakes one by one, and asked for volunteers to come and hold them. I was out of my seat like a shot, and found the warm, dry feel of the python quite a surprise when he draped it round my neck like a scarf. I mused on keeping one in my pump bag. But not for long. I don't think Mum could have coped with that. What she didn't seem to mind was that I wanted to take over the garden.

There was no thought at this time of anything so ambitious as 'design'. The shape of the garden didn't cross my mind. It didn't seem to cross anybody's. In our street, you had a bit of grass in the middle and a narrow border running round the edge. Up the posher end of town, they might have had a bit of crazy paving and a fish pond, but it never occurred to me that we should have them. What I did want was a greenhouse.

Buying one was out of the question. What if I made one? Just behind the stone-built midden at the end of the garden nearest the house was a patch of ground perhaps six feet by three that was sheltered by its wall. It seemed to catch the early-morning sun, and I could sneak a homemade greenhouse in there without it being seen from the house.

'Mam?'

'What is it now?'

'Can I build a greenhouse?'

'Where?'

'The other side of the midden?'

'How big?'

'Not very.'

'What do you want it for?'

'To grow a few plants in. Cookie says she'll give me some spider plants and some busy Lizzies – cuttings from hers in the front room. But I need somewhere to grow them.'

Mum looked sceptical. 'What are you going to make it from?'

I shrugged. 'Some bits of wood from the garden – there's that pile Dad's got. For firewood. I could use that.'

'What about glass?'

'I won't use glass. I'll use polythene.' I could see her about to interrupt, so I got in first. 'I've saved up my pocket money. I've got enough for the polythene. I've measured up. I need about twelve feet of it because it comes folded in half and it measures three feet wide, which means that when you unfold it, it's six feet wide, and I don't need a door because I can just make a flap, so can I do it, then?'

I saw her trying not to smile and knew that I'd won.

'Go on, then. But I don't want mess all over the garden.'

Triumphantly, that Saturday morning, I walked down the road to Hothersall's ironmonger's shop in Leeds Road and asked Mr Hothersall for four yards of polythene. Mr Hothersall always looked beleaguered, as if he had something more important he should be doing. I suppose this was understandable when he was serving a ten-year-old boy with a cheap bit of polythene and being asked to make his cut particularly straight. I never knew why he wore glasses. He was always looking over them, or had them pushed up on the top of his head. His black hair was slicked back with Brylcreem and he wore a tweed jacket and a tie and puffed a lot. You could never really hear what he was saying. He just sort of chuntered.

He put down the large pair of scissors and rolled up the polythene. 'Will that be all, young man?'

'Yes thank you.'

'That'll be three shillings, then, and I must get on.'

I handed over the cash and carried out the roll of polythene under my arm. It felt smooth and silky. I smelled it. It was a clean, healthy smell. The smell of growth. At least, that's what I would come to associate it with.

The sun was shining when I got back home. I went down to the cellar and found a hammer and a saw and some three-inch nails, and

for the rest of the day, barely stopping for lunch, I hammered and
sawed and built a small lean-to framework behind the midden.

'Can I borrow your dressmaking scissors?' I asked Mum.

'No you can't. They'll never cut anything again if you use them
on that. Ask your dad.'

Dad was up in the bathroom, plumbing in the hot water cylinder
and boxing it in so that Mum would have an airing cupboard as well
as radiators.

'Have you got any scissors, Dad?'

'What would I want scissors for?'

'Cutting things.'

He sighed. 'Hang on.' His blowlamp roaring all the while, he
rummaged in the brown canvas tool bag on the floor, and in
between the brass elbows and the offcuts of copper piping, he
found a lethal-looking knife. 'Be careful with it. It's sharp.'

It wasn't, but I took the warning, and in spite of its bluntness it cut
through the polythene as if through butter.

It was a simple matter to drawing-pin the polythene to the timber,
and within an hour I had created a secluded world all of my own. I
walked inside it and let down the flap that was to act as a door. The
noise of the back lane faded away. Even the birdsong was muffled.
Here inside my very own greenhouse was a place to escape. No one
else would come here. It was my own kingdom. I could put things
where I wanted them. I rigged up staging from old floorboards and
bricks, and went up to the lavatory on the landing to bring down the
half-dozen plants I had been growing on its windowsill – the cacti
and succulents from Mr Rhodes.

Harry Rhodes was the kindliest of teachers. Where others were
gruff and called boys by their surname, Mr Rhodes used Christian
names for boys and girls alike and smiled a lot. Mr Rhodes, with his
Roman nose and wire-rimmed spectacles, seemed always to be
optimistic and encouraging.

We all liked him because he was in charge of the gramophone
when Miss Hickinson walked into morning assembly. Usually he
would choose a stately bit of Handel's *Water Music*, but sometimes,
with a twinkle in his eye, he would play 'The Arrival of the Queen

of Sheba', to see if she would notice. She usually did, and shot him a warning sideways glance. He would sheepishly lift the needle from the groove, say in a dignified voice, 'Hands together and eyes closed,' and stand to attention while Miss Hickinson intoned the first prayer of morning assembly.

Mr Rhodes's hobby was growing cacti and succulents, which he did, by repute, in *two* greenhouses in Parklands, a rather smart crescent in Ben Rhydding.

It was from Mr Rhodes that I learned my first Latin name – *Bryophyllum pinnatum*. This succulent was memorable for another reason: it produces tiny plantlets on the edges of its leaves.

'You'll only have to buy this once, Alan,' said Mr Rhodes from behind his house plant stall at the church bazaar.

'Why's that, sir?'

'Look at all these little things here . . .' He pointed around the edge of the leaves. 'They're all babies. Every one will make a new plant.'

I'm not sure that I believed him, but I handed over my sixpence, and when his prophecy turned out to be true, Mr Rhodes became a god.

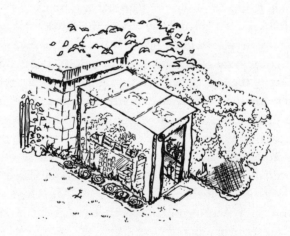

Cookie was true to her word and handed over a generous amount of cuttings of this and that, so that by the middle of summer my greenhouse was awash with geraniums and busy Lizzies, spider plants and false castor-oil palms.

But the interest in natural history continued unabated, and I bought from the pet shop a mouse. At one shilling and sixpence it was the cheapest thing on offer. I had given up hope of ever having a shed filled with hutches of rabbits and guinea pigs and hamsters, and thought that instead I could combine my hobbies of gardening and nature by keeping small animals in among my plants.

The idea lasted all of three days. On the fourth day next door's cat got in through the polythene flap of the door and frightened the mouse to death. I found it in its cage, quite stiff with rigor mortis.

Two things happened that day: I fitted a proper door to the greenhouse, and I decided that plants were a better bet than animals.

The Yorkshire Dales are not especially noted for their horticultural prowess. They have some great gardens, but commercial horticulture is thin on the ground in an area better suited to sheep and grouse. I suppose this makes it all the more surprising that I chose a career in gardening. But it was already in the blood. Both my father's father and his grandfather had been 'jobbing gardeners' – taking on gardening maintenance wherever they happened to live.

I never knew 'Granda', as he was always referred to, by way of distinguishing him from 'Grandad' – Mum's dad. He had died before I was born. There are pictures of him in the family album – a short, slim man with a moustache and a fine head of hair. I'm grateful to him for that. Dad seldom spoke about his father, except to say that he had died young.

Neither did Dad mention, in my early years, that his father had been a gardener, but that must have accounted for his reluctance to encourage me. He relented later on and gave in to the inevitable, but it must have worried him that in spite of his efforts to break the mould – when he became a plumber – that the urge to cultivate plants had not left the bloodline entirely.

I asked him, in later life, why he had never enjoyed gardening himself. 'Because my dad and grandad made me weed,' he said, 'and paid me a penny a bucket.' I'm glad that he did not work harder at putting me off.

Hopes and Dreams

W henever school got me down, I had one infallible way of lifting my spirits. I would dream. Not about cars and trains and space travel, but about having my own nursery. There were two role models in Ilkley, and both of them had all the ingredients necessary to allow my dreams full reign.

The first nursery was in an unlikely spot behind the police station. Mr Robertson was the proprietor, and you could see him busying himself among his plants wearing a tweed jacket and a faded blue apron, his dark hair slicked back with Brylcreem, a pencil and labels tucked into his top pocket, a budding knife in his horny hand.

There was no smartly painted sign proclaiming the nursery's ownership, or even its existence. You had to know it was there. But if you walked up the steep slope of Riddings Road, which rose towards the moor, and looked to your right just after the blue lamp, you would see a narrow gateway. The creaking iron gate opened into a small level area flanked by two wooden racks on which would be displayed bedding plants and vegetables, their prices chalked on to a small blackboard. There were scarlet geraniums in clay flower-pots, and fuchsias tumbling from troughs. Piles of apples were bought in to augment the home-grown produce, and there were fresh-dug potatoes and cabbages, too.

Beyond this pocket-sized sales floor, several stone steps led downwards to a long, low, white-painted greenhouse, which ran directly away from you into the distance. Through the open door, you could see solid staging – built of brick and topped with gravel – on which tray after tray of antirrhinums and tobacco plants, French marigolds and petunias would be fattening in the sun that filtered through the whitewashed panes – whitewashed to prevent sun scorch in the early days of May.

'Aye, it might look a bit shaded here, but you've got to watch that sun. It can burn 'em up in no time.'

Above the greenhouse and to its left was the open ground where Mr Robertson grew a few vegetables and the odd crop of fruit to add to the display on the wooden racks. There were shrubs here, too, in neat rows, and ornamental trees, to be dug up and sold in autumn when they were about to slip into their winter dormancy.

The scene was one of quiet productivity, and in the greenhouse the smell was one of growth – a mixture of foliage, damp earth, nicotine solution and Growmore. Step down into Mr Robertson's greenhouse, if you were lucky enough to be allowed – 'Aye, go on, then; come and 'ave a look' – and you could transport yourself into a world of bonemeal and bees, horse manure and heliotrope. For a young lad with green fingers – for that's what they told me I had – this was the stuff that dreams were made on.

The other nursery had a more picturesque location down by the Old Bridge that crosses the River Wharfe at the bottom of Stockeld Road. It's a handsome stone structure, built in 1675, and nestling beside it, right on the riverbank, is the Old Bridge Nursery. It is still there, though a lot smarter now, with plants brought in from another nursery lower down the dale. But when I was a boy, it was a 'proper' nursery that grew its own plants, with a little lean-to greenhouse and a stone potting shed on whose door were marked the heights of the various floods.

Running this nursery has always been a precarious business, for the Wharfe breaks its banks every few years and plants are quite likely to be uprooted and carried off downstream when the waters are in full spate.

Arthur Baxter would work here in between doing another job. You could see him at the weekends – a burly, fair-haired man in baggy khaki shorts and a singlet if the weather was warm – planting wallflowers and sweet williams for autumn sale in the raised beds of dark alluvial earth that he'd built to accommodate them. He'd be bent double among the rows with a trowel, picking his way carefully between the plants in his large hobnailed boots.

He grew alpines in white plastic drinking cups and sold them for a few pence each. Anyone in Ilkley who had just made a rockery with lumps of local stone could plant it up for a couple of pounds with Arthur's generously priced alpines.

It seemed to me an idyllic existence. Arthur never said much. He seemed rather shy. But he'd smile and offer advice if you asked, to make sure that you had success with your plants when you got them home.

The two nurseries inspired me to open my own. I had no money, and anyway, I was far too young to have a 'proper' nursery, but the garden, and my polythene greenhouse, seemed like a good start.

I found a piece of timber in Dad's supply of offcuts in the cellar, brought home as kindling wood for the fire in the front room, and I made a sign with my Flowmaster felt-tip pen. 'Corncrake Nursery,' it said, and I nailed it to our rickety garden gate.

I might have joined the Wharfedale Naturalists' Society, but I'd never seen a corncrake. I didn't even know what one looked like. But it sounded right – country-like and rural – and it gave our tiny back garden an air of importance.

I did broach the subject of having beds of earth where I could grow things in rows and sell them come the autumn, but Mum was too partial to her hydrangea to allow me to do that, and she also liked the patch of grass on which she could park her kitchen buffet on sunny days for her morning cup of milky coffee. You couldn't do that between rows of wallflowers and sweet williams.

So I settled, instead, for growing pot plants in my greenhouse, and taking more cuttings of Cookie's spider plants and coleuses and busy Lizzies. I decided round about now that I would be a gardener when I grew up. It was really the only thing I was good at, and the enjoyment of raising my own plants gave me a thrill that nothing else could match.

Mum said, 'I think you should be a propagator.'

I wasn't at all sure what a propagator was, but thought that it sounded a bit technical.

Mum said, 'He's someone who grows plants from cuttings and seeds. Someone who raises plants.'

I liked the sound of that, but thought that with a name like 'propagator' it might turn out to be a bit beyond me. I'd be happy just being a gardener.

I told my dad that evening.

'What do you want to be a gardener for?'

'Because I like it.'

He didn't look convinced. 'I think you'd be better off with a trade.'

'But gardening *is* a trade,' I protested.

'I don't think you can get very far, though. And there's not much money in it.'

I let the matter rest. There was no point in carrying on. Anyway, Dad hadn't said no, he'd just not sounded very encouraging. And now he was reading his paper.

I went back out into the garden and tried to think of a way of making my nursery pay. Perhaps then I could prove to Dad that there was money in it. But as yet I had nothing to sell – only the plants that I would be able to take cuttings from, and if I sold those I'd have nothing. It seemed as though I was stuck.

And then I noticed the mint. Apart from the 'Dorothy Perkins' that grew over the chain-link fence at the end of the garden, it was the only plant that really thrived in our garden. (Even Mum's hydrangea had a bit of a struggle.) There was a great swathe of mint growing out from the privet hedge, and it was spearmint – the tangy sort that nips at your nose when you squeeze it between your fingers. I checked it for holes. It was fairly clean without too much slug or caterpillar damage, and it had grown to about a foot high now. Yes, that would do.

I made an amendment to my sign. In the gap below 'Corncake Nursery' I wrote in felt-tip pen 'Mint 1d a bunch'. I stood back to

admire my handiwork. It wasn't the neatest piece of sign writing but as it was already nailed to the gate it would have to do.

The following morning I got up early to do my watering in the little greenhouse, and left for school at half past eight, checking with Mum that she would be in all day if I had any customers for the mint.

'What do you want me to do?' she asked.

'It's a penny a bunch. I've put a tobacco tin by the gate.'

'All right, go on, then, get off.'

All day I wondered what I would find when I came home. A tin full of pennies might be being a bit optimistic, but three or four pence would be handy. At least it would buy a few seeds and allow me to increase my stock a bit faster. And it was the time for new potatoes, so people would need mint to drop in the pan when they cooked them. I congratulated myself on this piece of logic. It seemed that my timing was perfect. The mint was also growing fast at this time of year and would quickly renew itself.

Through maths and composition I speculated on the outcome. At ten to four, I bounded out of school and up the road to check on my success.

Before I climbed the back steps to the kitchen, I dropped my bag and opened the garden gate. The tin was not there. And neither was the mint. It had all gone. There was no sign of it at all. Crikey! So many people must have wanted it that we had run out. The tin would have been so full of pennies that my mum must have taken it inside for safe keeping.

I jumped down the garden steps and bounded in through the back door to find Mum. She was standing over the stove, stirring a pan of custard. I was surprised that she didn't look a bit happier, bearing in mind how successful we had been.

'Did a lot of people come?' I asked.

'No,' she said, without looking up.

'But the mint. It's all gone.'

'I know.' She raised her eyes and lifted the pan of custard off the gas. 'Sorry, Sparrow. I'm afraid we had a bit of a disaster.'

I wondered what could have happened. Normally it was I who had the disasters, not Mum.

'What do you mean?'

'Well,' she said, pouring the hot custard over a bowl of sliced bananas, 'you know Mr Wright – from the bottom house on the other side of the road?'

I confirmed that I did. Billy Wright was about ninety and was always busy doing something – mending people's fences or garden gates, or digging a patch of their gardens for a few bob. You could see him at all hours in his orange-brown bib-and-brace overalls, worn navy-blue jacket and flat cap, pushing his bike to his next location. He had a squeaky voice and a white moustache, and spoke in such a broad Yorkshire accent that sometimes you could hardly understand him.

'Well, Mr Wright came and knocked on the door and said, "Is it right that your lad's selling mint?"'

'What did you say?'

'I said that yes, you were, but that as it grew so easily I didn't think you'd really want to charge him a penny a bunch.'

'Oh, Mum!'

'Now don't interrupt. Mr Wright said that he wanted some, but that it was only right he should pay the going rate. So he gave me the penny.' She put her hand into the pocket of her pinny, pulled out the penny, and handed it to me. 'Here you are.'

I took the coin and turned it over in my hand. It was, indeed, a penny. A single penny.

'But the whole clump has gone.'

Mum looked apologetic. 'I know. Tight old so-and-so. I suppose I should have stood over him while he took it, but I never thought. He dug up the whole clump and took it to plant in somebody's garden.'

And so it was that any commercial horticultural aspirations I might have had evaporated on that one summer's day, thanks to Billy Wright and the disappearing mint.

I decided, in the end, that if I wanted to be a gardener, then I might as well do it for the love of it, rather than for any significant financial gain. My dad came round to the idea in the end, but I can't help thinking that the Billy Wright episode proved he had a point.

The Wharfedale Music Festival is famed locally for its high standard of musicianship and the fact that it is a great showcase for local talent. I never appeared there, though I did help out each year as a parks department apprentice, with the floral decorations at the front of the stage.

Occasionally, on the last night, there would be a family outing to hear the finalists perform and to join in with the singing of 'Jerusalem' – my dad always singing loud enough to embarrass my sister and me.

That I never learned to play the piano is a lifelong regret, and I lay the blame fairly and squarely at the feet of my mother.

The Piano

We never had the luxury of a hallway. Not on our side of the street. Our front door opened directly on to the sitting room, which meant that when the wind was in the west, Dad's newspaper could be blown out of his hands. For the first few years a sideboard stood against the left-hand wall as you came in. Somewhere to drop the keys in a glass bowl next to the clock. It was a graceless sort of coffin-on-legs; a treacly dark oak with sculpted fleur-de-lys motifs of dull copper attached to the two doors at either end – a nod in the direction of William Morris. But only a slight one. It lasted about as long as most of the furniture in our house, thanks to the proximity of Dacre, Son & Hartley's saleroom at the bottom of the street. After a couple of years, three at most, my mother would decide it was time for a change, and swap a set of chairs, a table or a sideboard for something new, which was actually old.

These changes usually happened in spring, when the sun sneaked over the slate roofs of the houses opposite for the first time, slanting in through the kitchen window and highlighting the swirling motes of silvery dust in the air that her lavender furniture polish had failed to capture. Like Mole in *The Wind in the Willows*, Mum would feel the pull of the outside world, which translated itself into a change of scene inside.

These bouts of spring fever would be preceded by a sort of restlessness. 'Alan,' she would say to my father, 'these chairs are getting really tired,' and she'd point to some patch of wear on the arms, or watch as my father would nail back one of the long supporting springs that had come adrift from the wooden frame of a more 'contemporary' easy chair, allowing the seat cushion to slither halfway to the floor while the occupant clung on to the wooden arms for dear life.

My parents were never great movers. Apart from the couple of uncomfortable years with my father's mother when they first got married, and their first house in Nelson Road a year after I was born in 1950, the move up to a pebble-dashed semi in the smarter end of town in 1965 was their last. But my mother made up for this lack of daring in the housing stakes when it came to furniture. Everything from Ercol to reproduction Carolean, from arts and crafts to G-Plan graced our front room over the years. You would just get used to the shape of one chair and adjust your posture to suit, when another appeared, but the most dramatic change of all was the replacement of the ugly sideboard that nobody liked with a piano.

Quite how Mother managed these changeovers is unclear. There would never be a gap where one piece had been removed while we waited for another to appear. No. We would go to school in the morning and when we came home the change of scene would have been achieved as if by magic. From our point of view at any rate. We were spared the frantic scenes of removal men staggering out of the front door with one piece of furniture and carting it off down the bottom of the street in the morning, and then staggering up with something to replace it in the afternoon, but that's what must have happened.

The sales were held once a fortnight in the Victoria Hall Saleroom at the junction of Nelson Road and Little Lane. It's still there, a facelift or two later. Mother would hardly miss a sale, doing her best to keep the family home in good shape, and vying with other ladies of the town for the best pieces. Not that she was ever into antiques or remotely knowledgeable about them. To her, the word 'antique' was a euphemism for 'second-hand'. Mum had grown up with too much 'junk' to ever be enamoured of things that were old. She'd have bought brand new if she could have afforded it, and in later life her house was full of teak, rather than mahogany, but for the first twenty years of their marriage, new was out of the question, so she'd brave the salerooms and try to avoid the likes of Mrs Hatch – 'I'm looking for some superior carpeting; I'm tired of my Wilton,' was one reported remark.

Only beds and prams were bought new back then. The rest – sofas and chairs, sideboards and tables, bicycles and blanket boxes – all came from the saleroom. Today, it was a piano.

It would have been moved by the two brown-coated men employed by the auctioneers: the loping, ever-cheery and bespectacled John Freeman with his daily greeting – ''Ello, young Alan. Have you started plumbing yet?' (As my father was a plumber, the question never varied. If I met him tomorrow, I've no doubt that the question would be the same) – and the older, lugubrious Teddy Woodrup, who muttered a lot but said little. I picture them heaving the instrument up the gravelly road to our house. It would be a steep climb for a piano, especially on one of those little two-wheeled trollies they used. There would be John shouting instructions at one end and Teddy grumbling at the other, tilting the piano this way and that, puffing and swearing under his breath (I don't think John knew the words), and finally manhandling the instrument, to the accompaniment of assorted twangs and zither-like chords, up the three stone steps that led into the front room.

When Kath and I came home from school, there it was, sitting against the wall, threateningly. The only thing I liked about it were the two brass candlesticks that jutted out from the front. I thought they gave the front room a touch of class. Mum didn't agree. 'They're too ostentatious,' she said, and removed them one day while I was at school.

I always wanted to like that piano, but it did its best to intimidate me. To be fair, it was not as large as some upright pianos. It was what my mother called a 'cottage grand'. It seemed a grandiose title for an upright piano, especially one that lacked candlesticks, and it seemed to give our stone terraced house an extra air of gentility. It was of highly figured walnut; the plush-covered mahogany stool did not match.

There was never any mention of my being allowed to play it. Instead, lessons were booked for my sister. When I asked my mother in later life why I was not given the opportunity of discovering whether I was a pianist in the making, her reply was brief: 'You'd never have practised.'

My mother could play, but she had a sort of vamping style that made one piece of music sound exactly the same as another. She played by ear. You could hum a tune and she could instantly play it back to you – invariably with the same rhythm, and with the same sort of movement of her hands – the lower one would play one chord in the centre of the keyboard, and then one down at the bottom end, then back to the middle and so on. Her movements never varied. She looked like someone miming playing the piano, but music did come out of it.

My father could play one piece only. He would sit at the piano, crouch over it, and with his thick plumber's fingers bent to resemble the legs of fat spiders, he would play the first few bars of a deeply resonant sonata that I can still hear in my head but to this day I have heard nowhere else. It has, for the last ten years at least, been totally ignored by both Radio 3 and Classic FM. He only knew the first dozen bars or so, and then it fizzled out. He would smile to himself, pleased that he had been able to recall even that after a gap of perhaps twenty years, and go back to his paper.

Kath agreed to the piano lessons with little more than a murmur of reluctance, and into our lives came the elegant figure of Mrs Clayton. She wore floral-print dresses and rimless spectacles and spoke posh, which was a bit of a surprise as she lived nearer Leeds than we did. Mrs Clayton charged seven shillings and sixpence for three-quarters of an hour and was engaged in preference to the more local Miss Martin, who charged five shillings for half an hour. This, maintained my mother, was much better value. Maths had never been my strong point and I presumed that I was missing something.

Every Tuesday evening, as soon as school was finished, Kath would come home and perch on the piano stool with Mrs Clayton at her left elbow, offering encouragement and pointing at the little tadpoles that were swimming between the lines on the pages of music.

Kath never learned what the pedals were for. Her musical career was over before she grew tall enough to reach them, though she did manage to win a medal at the Wharfedale Music Festival in the trio section. She would sit there, night after night, frowning over some tricky piece of fingering, her little feet with the white ankle socks and peep-toe sandals dangling in mid-air.

Mrs Clayton would have earnest conversations with my mother at the kitchen door while she drank her cup of tea and ate the sandwiches she had brought, wrapped in greaseproof paper in a neat little box. It was 'Fanny Waterman this' and 'Malcolm Sargent that' every Tuesday night outside our kitchen.

Having regaled my mother with her week's musical exploits, she'd go on to her next engagement with a girl who was always described as 'my most promising pupil'. It was a title Kath was unlikely to inherit. One evening, alone in the house and waiting for Mrs Clayton to arrive, she set all the clocks a quarter of an hour fast – the sitting-room clock, the kitchen clock, she even adjusted the clocks on the bedside tables in case the teacher spotted them on the way to the toilet on the first-floor landing. Mrs Clayton finished a quarter of an hour early and Kath ran around the house resetting the clocks.

But there was a flaw in the plan. Kath had not thought it through. Mum returned a few minutes before Mrs Clayton should have left, to find the music teacher gone and Kath sitting at the piano alone, her tongue sticking out between her teeth, the better to concentrate. Nothing was said, but relations between Mum and Mrs Clayton the following week were a touch frosty. If the lessons were only going to last half an hour, why didn't we have Miss Martin and save half a crown?

Sometimes when Kath was practising, the family next door would be stung into action. The MacDonalds were only there for a year. They had two children. Adam was about my age, and we messed around together down the back. His older sister, Moira, had long, dark hair worn in plaits. It was she who played the harmonium that sat with its back to the same wall as our new piano.

Within moments of Kath opening the lid and running her fingers through some hesitant scales or arpeggios, the wheeze of the harmonium could be heard through the plaster. I think Moira only knew one tune, but she could play it until the cows came home. 'Doh, ray, me, fah, soh, lah, te, doh' would tinkle out on our side of the wall, and 'The Bluebells of Scotland' would be the homesick dirge that filtered through from number 35. Not that we called it 'The Bluebells of Scotland'. It was known as 'Oh, where, tell me where', because that was what my mother would sing, clearly more impressed with Moira's playing than that of her daughter. 'Oh, where, tell me where is your Highland laddie gone? He's gone wi' streaming banners where noble deeds are done. And it's oh, in my heart I wish him safe at home.'

I did not realise then the significance of the lyrics. Before she married my father, three years after the war, Mum had been 'involved' with a Scot by the name of John Douglas. 'Uncle John' and his sister, 'Auntie Ella', lived in Galashiels. We saw them maybe once a year when they came down for their annual holiday in Morecambe. Uncle John had lost a leg in the war, and I think Mum had met him when he was convalescing. He had a false leg fitted and walked with a stick, and when they met, Mum would often walk with her arm in his along the prom at Morecambe, with me and Kath dawdling behind with Dad and Auntie Ella. There was always a spark between Mum and Uncle John. A twinkle in his eye. A fondness in her look. My father never alluded to it, and eventually, by the time I was into my thirties, Mum and Uncle John had lost touch. I suppose she just let it go, probably to my father's relief. But in the late 1950s, there was always a wistfulness about her when she asked, 'Oh, where, tell me where is your Highland laddie gone?' Even if Galashiels hardly ranks as the Highlands.

There were times, when nobody was in, that I would open the lid of the piano and finger the keys. Maybe if I thought hard about a piece of piano music I had heard – something played by Winifred Attwell, or Joe 'Mr Piano' Henderson on *The Billy Cotton Band Show* – I'd be able to play it myself. Perhaps it was all down to intense concentration. Something my mother never thought I had. I tried the technique. It didn't work, and the piano was, and remains, a mystery.

If it were not for two things, I would have little affection for it at all. The first was a distant cousin. She was called Linda, and had come down to Ilkley from Beverley to visit some other member of the family. They didn't have a piano, and her mother, anxious that she should keep up her technique while on holiday, had asked if she could use ours on which to practise.

I came home from school one evening to find this blonde vision sitting at our piano and playing like an angel. She looked like an angel, too, her soft bob framing a face with the most melting smile I had ever seen.

It was love at first sight – or so I convinced myself. In my imagination we packed our spare clothes in her music case – a proper one with a shiny metal rod that held the flap in place – and ran away to be together for ever on a desert island where I'd make dens and cook things over a campfire, and she'd play the piano under a palm tree.

I suppose I must have been eleven or twelve at the time. Aware of girls and aware of beauty, but so far uninvolved with either. We had a brief but self-conscious conversation. I could tell that she liked me. There was something in her manner; in the way that she fluttered her eyelashes and looked away when she talked to me. I liked her, too. We spoke again the following week when she came back for the last time. I have not seen her since. I remember only my mother's disapproval of any further contact, but whether this was due to some smouldering family feud (none of them serious, but each one carefully observed) or the inadvisability of fraternisation between distant cousins I don't know. We did swap letters, though. Two or three of them. And that was it.

The second and most lasting thing that piano taught me was how to drive a car, several years before I was old enough to get a licence. I found a book in the local library. It recommended that in order to teach yourself the finer points of changing gear, you would need three things: a walking stick, a flowerpot and a piano.

The idea was that you sat at the piano and treated the three pedals as the accelerator, brake and clutch. You turned the flowerpot upside down on the floor to the left of the piano stool and pushed the end of the walking stick through the hole. It became the gear lever. (There was no suggestion in the book that the technique

could actually be practised in a stationary car; few people had cars, most people had a piano.)

I followed the directions and, night after night, sat at the wheel of our cottage grand in the front room, until the sound of my revving irritated my father enough for him to suggest that I put the 'car' in the garage and go to bed.

The piano disappeared at the same time as Kath's enthusiasm, Mrs Clayton and my mother's urge for a new piece of furniture. I never did learn to play it, but I can double-declutch with the best of them.

My inability to get out of doing something I don't want to has been a lifelong curse. Most folk are sensible enough to smile sweetly, politely decline an unappealing offer, then turn and walk away. I am more likely to miss the moment at which withdrawal can be managed gracefully and end up hurtling headlong into the abyss of embarrassment because of my unwillingness to offend or disappoint. Which is a long-winded way of saying that I am the male equivalent of Ado Annie in Oklahoma *— I'm just a guy who can't say no. It has been thus ever since I was small.*

Street Theatre

T he rough lane that sloped past the back of our row of terraced houses, between the dwellings and their short, narrow gardens, was known, with that classic northern capacity for stating the obvious, as 'the back'. It was almost entirely un-made-up; a rough and uneven compaction of native soil and the ashes from fireplaces and back boilers that had been dumped on it at the dawn of every day for over a hundred years – apart from the patch behind Mr Barker's house.

The Barkers were a childless couple, and Mr Barker, apart from being a special constable and wearing white sleeves over his navy-blue tunic when he directed the traffic on the gasworks corner on bank holidays, seemed to have more time on his hands than most of the dads. As a result, the bit of back outside his house was concreted. Not evenly, in one great slab, but in sections that he had laid bit by bit – when he had the time, the inclination and the few bob necessary to invest in another bag of cement.

By the time I was eight or nine, the Barkers' bit of back was entirely of hard standing. The mums liked it because it was the one stretch of ground they could walk on without sinking up to their ankles in wet weather when they were wearing stilettos, and the kids liked it because it was a good place to play games that needed an even surface.

Occasionally Mrs Barker – a martyr to headaches – would have a bit of a turn and come out and live up to her name, shouting at us to clear off and wringing her hands under her pinny when we got on her nerves, but for most of the time she didn't seem to mind us being there.

I don't know whose idea it was initially, but the upshot was that 'Barkers' Square', as it came to be known (all ten feet of it), would make the perfect performance area.

At the very mention of the word 'performance', you couldn't see Mickey Hudson, Dokey Gell or Robert Petty for dust. They were down by the bus-garage wall kicking an empty baked-bean can. There remained Pauline Cawood, Virginia Petty (Robert's older sister), Jane Evans, Philomena Forrest and the only lad in the street not given to causing offence. Me.

You can look at this in several ways: I was weak and feeble; I was trying to be helpful; I had an inbuilt desire to perform from an early age; or, far more likely, I had not fully considered the implications. You can rule out the fact that I was up for a snog. That particular use for a girl wouldn't occur to me for three or four years yet.

As I remember, I had my back to the wall. Literally and figuratively.

'You can be the master of ceremonies,' confided Jane Evans, stroking her bunches.

I liked the sound of being master of anything so I just shrugged.

'Yes,' agreed Philomena, the little one who bit her bottom lip when she hit you. 'You can announce us.'

'What are you going to do?' I asked.

Pauline whipped out a large picture book from behind her back. 'This.'

I leaned forward to look at the glossy jacket. It showed a photograph of a man and a woman, both wearing eye shadow and holding a strange pose. Then I read the title: *The Princess Book of Ballet.*

That should have been the moment. The moment at which I ran in the direction of the baked-bean can. But I didn't. I stayed rooted to the spot thanks to the natural curiosity that has helped widen my interests in all things cultural for a little over half a century.

Pauline opened the book and the other three grouped round her. I kept a safe distance.

'I like this one best,' said Jane, pointing to a picture of a man in tights who was holding a girl in a short net skirt above his head with one hand. ' "Paz de Dukes," ' she said.

'Yes, I like that one, too,' agreed Pauline.

'I'll be the man, and you be the woman,' said Jane.

Philomena kept quiet, probably relieved that being the shortest of the quartet, she wouldn't have to lift anybody up, never mind with one hand.

It was decided that Virginia, the blonde, would be in charge of the advertising break, where television commercials would be sung to give the others time to change their costumes.

I was a bit worried. I mean, what if Jane dropped Pauline head first on to the concrete of Barkers' Square? And there were technical and artistic considerations, too. Who would supply the music and the costumes? I might be unable to say no, but I've always been practical.

All of these doubts were brushed aside. 'We can find the costumes at home and I can bring my record player,' said Jane with a dismissive wave of her arm.

It was pretty clear that in spite of being the master of ceremonies, my role was subservient to those of the main performers. Even the advertisers. All I would have to do was provide the links. Talk while they changed their costumes. And turn on the record player.

The girls sat down in a circle and decided on the short programme. Jane and Pauline would perform the 'Paz de Dukes' from *Swan Lake* (Jane had the music for that so there was no problem there), and Philomena would do a short character dance of her own devising, with her dog, to whatever other bit of ballet music could be found.

Virginia would choose three commercials with jingles that could be sung during the brief intermission.

After consultation with Mr and Mrs Barker, the date was set for the following Friday. Oh, and another duty of the master of ceremonies would be to make the poster. The one that would be nailed to the Barkers' fence. Because I had the set of poster paints.

I remember being nervous that fateful morning, but it was too late now. The day dawned fine and fair, but I couldn't see how the brief programme would in any way attract mums from up and down the street to come and watch. Not when it was in competition with washing, ironing and getting 'him' his tea.

But come they did, and the motley collection of chairs from all the kitchens down our side of Nelson Road were pressed into service – pink ones with spoked backs, blue ones and chipped white ones, posh chrome bar stools with padded black vinyl seats, and even the odd rush-seated ladder-back found their way into three serried rows of seating.

We didn't charge – that would have been pushing it – but come two o'clock a good dozen and a half spectators had turned up to watch. Mainly mums, with the odd reluctant and bleary-eyed dad who was on shift work.

I'd found a white shirt and a red bow tie, and made my own clipboard from the back of a Kellogg's cornflakes packet and a bulldog clip. (Practical again, you see.) I strode out on to the square and announced the afternoon's performance: 'Ladies and gentlemen, welcome to Barkers' Square and this afternoon's ballet to be performed by Jane Evans and Pauline Cawood, with a speciality dance by Philomena Forrest and her dog, Laddie, and adverts by Virginia Petty.'

A ripple of polite applause followed and I began to feel optimistic.

'First, the "Paz de Dukes" from *Swan Lake*.' Except that it wasn't really the 'Paz de Dukes'. Jane and Pauline had thought the better of any form of lifting on concrete and settled instead for Jane playing both the handsome prince and the wicked von Rothbart with no discernible difference between the two.

I turned on the record player and lowered the needle. Pauline did try to start the performance to the sound of the Temperance Seven playing 'Pasadena', but decided, after a few bars, that it wasn't really the right rhythm, so I removed Mrs Cawood's favourite record, which she had clearly substituted for the Tchaikovsky, and tried again.

Better luck this time. To the soaring orchestral accompaniment, Pauline teetered on in her best white party frock with a pink sash and began to pirouette across the square, until she reached the privet at the other side and lost her balance. Having extracted herself from the hedge and brushed the dead leaves from her sleeve, she pirouetted off in the other direction and continued back and forth like this in dizzying motion until the music reached a dramatic crescendo.

At this point, Jane leaped noisily from the Barkers' outside toilet in a grey gymslip and V-neck sweater with a golden cloak over her shoulders. She jumped around the square in ever more gigantic leaps, propelled by a new pair of black plimsolls, and eventually paused to explain her actions. 'You will turn into a swan, now I will be gone!' she exclaimed. It was a brief performance. Pauline continued pirouetting, with no sign of any sort of transformation, and Jane disappeared back into the toilet and refused to come out. Nerves had got the better of her. As the music pounded on and Pauline was in serious danger of collapse due to an excess of pirouetting, I pleaded with Jane to vacate the privy. To no avail. Through the keyhole I could hear stifled sobs, while the music built to its grand finale.

I gave up on Jane, lifted the needle from the record and stepped forward to announce the intermission. It was not necessary. At that moment, powering their way sideways through the Barkers' garden gate and on to the square came Virginia and Philomena in a Tiller Girl formation of two, kicking up their legs and singing 'Have you tried Robinson's lemon barley, lemon fresh, barley smooth? If you haven't tried Robinson's lemon barley, well . . . you should!' And then, as if by design, they were lost from sight behind Mrs Barker's washing.

There was no more. Three adverts had been planned. Only one had materialised.

I stepped forward to announce the next act, only to see Philomena's dog, Laddie, rushing off up the back after the coalman with his owner in hot pursuit, biting her bottom lip in between yelling at him, 'Laddie! LADDIE! Come back here, you little bugger!' But Laddie had gone, and with him any hopes we might have had of a longer performance.

The first and last ballet to appear on Barkers' Square had lasted, at most, four minutes. But as the uncomplaining mothers lugged their furniture back into their kitchens, I did hear at least one of them describe the afternoon as 'unforgettable'.

Mickey Hudson, Dokey Gell and Robert Petty were still down by the bus garage wall kicking their tin can when I caught up with them. They said nothing. And for that I was deeply grateful.

Just in case a picture is emerging of a pathetic little wimp who was happier playing with his plants than a football (which I was) and with girls rather than boys (which I wasn't — well, not till later), I would like to point out that there were times when I could be ever-so-slightly daring.

I would climb trees for apples (one sprained wrist and two experiences of being winded), scale rocks on the moors with the agility of a gazelle (one sprained ankle), and wade across the River Wharfe (but only in summer when it was low).

My cricketing prowess was, it is true, limited, and my footballing skills even less worthy of note, but when it came to a vivid imagination, I was never found wanting. Sometimes, though, with the encouragement of mates in the street, things did get a bit out of hand.

Playing With Fire

W e'd done all the things you normally do – played kick-can
down the bottom of the street and cricket with a tennis ball
against the bus-garage wall, and we'd no money to go and buy seeds
from Woolies to sow in Mickey's back garden, so the two of us
decided to have a fire.

That was the great thing about Mickey's back garden. Unlike
ours, on the other side of Nelson Road, which backed on to the
gardens of the houses in Wellington Road, Mickey's back garden
was surrounded by old stone buildings that were used by a local
builder for storing stuff. There were no windows in the sides that
faced on to the garden, and the hedge at the bottom was too thick to
allow anyone walking down the back lane to see in.

The additional perk was that both Mickey's parents worked – his
mum, Dorothy, in a newsagent and his dad, Stan, in a greengrocer's,
so there was never anyone around to say no.

As parents go, Mickey's seemed amazingly relaxed compared with
mine. They never enquired what he had been doing all day. They
also seemed better off. They smoked Kensitas cigarettes, and
collected the coupons; as a result of which, Mickey and his sister,
Janet, always seemed to have new bikes. I tried to persuade my dad
to change brands, but he wouldn't. He said he preferred Senior
Service, and anyway, Mum thought gift coupons were a bit
suspicious. You never got something for nothing, she said. But
the bikes seemed real enough to me.

We rode down to the land at the back of the salerooms on them –
he on his Raleigh Palm Beach, and me on my little maroon Hercules
that we'd got from someone in the scout group who'd grown out of

it. We parked the bikes by the railings and sneaked through a gap in the wire netting into the area known as Mennell's Yard.

We weren't really supposed to be in there – it was a builder's yard full of piles of sand and aggregate; sacks of hardened cement that they couldn't be bothered to throw away and broken paving slabs. The men came in the morning to load up their lorry and van, but they were usually gone by nine o'clock, so we had the place to ourselves.

We could sculpt massive desert scenes in the pile of sand and take our model soldiers there to stage battles between the British army and Rommel's Afrika Korps, until I got fed up with always being German and arranged for a landslide to engulf the lot.

Along one side of the yard was an open-sided shed covered in corrugated iron. It was used by the salerooms as a dumping ground for stuff that was broken or too shoddy even to be sold in a job lot; the junk from house clearances that nobody would give even a tanner for. As I said, we weren't really supposed to be in there, but John Freeman and Teddy Woodrup, the only folk likely to disturb us, turned a blind eye, as long as we didn't make too much noise or cause too much trouble. When the yard was empty, we could do what we liked.

'Look over here . . .' Mickey was crouching over an old tea chest. It was full of wood wool. 'This'll do as kindling.'

'We can't start a fire here.' I heard the words of caution coming out of my mouth and felt a bit lame.

'Not here. Back in the garden, daft bugger. Stuff some in your pockets.'

So I did. Then I climbed a pile of broken floor tiles that started slithering to the ground in a ceramic avalanche.

'Shurrup! They'll hear us.'

I came down gingerly and went to explore another corner of the shed. I found two things: an old bentwood chair with a cane seat that had collapsed and the top half of a statue of a knight on horseback.

'Here! Look at this!' I called Mickey over.

'Aw, wow!'

'Good i'n't it!'

Mickey lifted it out of my hands. 'It's heavy. It must be made of lead. You know what you can do with lead?'

'What?'

'You can melt it and make it into other things.'

'Shall we take it?'

Mickey looked around. 'Yeah. It's broken. It's just been chucked away. Nobody'll want it.'

I couldn't argue. The statue, which looked like a poor copy of the Anglia television knight in shining armour, was only about six inches high, and the bottom half of the horse was missing. It had obviously been dumped. So, too, had the chair. Aside from the missing seat, it was also suffering from woodworm. One of the legs was about to fall off.

Mickey took the knight, and I took the chair, and we cycled the hundred yards or so back to his garden as nonchalantly as we could.

Once there, we unloaded our plunder and set to to make the fire. There were plenty of places to choose from. There were no obvious flower beds or borders, not even an obvious lawn. There would be patches where, when the mood took him, Mickey would fork over a bit of the black, ash-filled soil, surround the irregular-shaped bed with broken bricks and small boulders yielded during the cultivation of the earth, and sow clarkia or marigolds, godetia or love-in-a-mist, but that was during the summer months; at other times of year the ground was a featureless wasteland, interrupted only by a few clumps of nettles and the finest stand of Japanese knotweed in the street. Its hollow stems made great pea-shooters. But today we had other fish to fry.

We settled on a spot of flattened mud roughly halfway down the garden. The wood wool was piled up and a couple of broken Fyffe's banana boxes filched from the outhouse where Stan Hudson kept his rejects.

We cracked the thin timber over our knees and piled it on the wood wool, then we went inside the house to look for matches. Mickey found some on the mantelpiece, along with a packet of cigarettes. 'Do you want one?' he asked.

I shook my head.

'I've got these . . .' He offered me another box of cigarettes. Sweet ones, made of sugar icing, with pink ends. At the age of eight or nine they seemed preferable to the real thing, and we stuck them in our mouths and leaned on the mantelpiece, pretending to smoke and to swear as best we could.

'Bloody buggers,' said Mickey.

'Bloody buggering buggers,' I responded.

We amused ourselves for ten minutes or so like this, pretending to be old men, tired of life and cursing everything around us, until our cigarettes had been munched down to the stubs. Then we swallowed our fag ends and went out with the matches to light our fire.

It took hold straightaway, the flames fanned by a gentle breeze. Soon, the banana crates were ashes, and we needed thicker timber to keep the fire alight. We hauled a couple of old tree stumps from the bottom of the privet hedge and lobbed them into the middle of the dying flames so that a plume of sparks shot up into the sky. They must have been quite dry, because they took hold quickly, and we warmed ourselves by the flames.

Soon, even they had died down, and Mickey suggested that the embers were now hot enough to melt the lead. He found an old paint tin, still encrusted with the green colouring of their back door, and set it on the hot fire bed, watching the remains of the paint bubbling and sizzling in the bottom of the tin. Eventually, when the paint had turned to ashes, he lifted up the battered knight and dropped it into the tin. Miraculously, before our eyes, the dull grey soldier began to melt and turned, instead, to shining liquid.

'It's not lead,' I offered, 'it's silver!'

'Nah!' said Mickey, clearly experienced in lead foundry. 'It always does that. It's just molten lead.'

I was enormously impressed at his knowledge, especially when he fetched an empty baked-bean tin from their outhouse. With the aid of a couple of sticks he managed to pour the molten lead from the larger can into the smaller one, which he used as a mould, and a few minutes later he tipped out a perfect cylinder of shiny lead.

'That's magic!' I said, scared of Mickey's alchemy, if I was honest, but also deeply impressed.

We kicked the lead ingot around a bit until it cooled, then lifted it and marvelled at its weight in relation to its bulk. And then we got bored.

The fire was still glowing, and the broken chair was lying unused a few feet away.

I saw Mickey's mind whirring. 'You know that film we saw at the flicks on Saturday?'

I shook my head.

'Aw, no. You di'n't cum, did you?'

'No.' I never went to the pictures on a Saturday afternoon. Not unless it was raining. My mum wouldn't let me. 'Go out and get some fresh air. You don't want to be stuck in there when it's fine.'

And I didn't, to be honest; I'd rather be out playing – down by the river or in the garden or the woods. But it was easier to say that my mum wouldn't let me – that way, they'd be sympathetic, rather than having a go.

'Well, any road, there were this cowboy, and he were tryin' to rescue this girl from this baddy, and the baddy ties him to a chair and lights a fire under it.'

I could see where the conversation was leading.

'Did he escape?'

'Oh, yeah. He just wriggled about a bit while the flames were sort of lickin' up' is legs and eventually they burned through the rope and he got away.'

'Oh.'

'Do you fancy tryin' it?'

I knew what the answer was before I asked the question. 'Who goes in the chair?'

Mickey found the rope in the outhouse along with the broken banana crates and the old paint tins, as I knew he would. He tied my feet securely to the legs of the chair and bound my hands behind me on the bentwood frame.

Obediently I helped him position me in the centre of the fire by shuffling forward into the middle of the hot ashes, and like a Yorkshire version of Joan of Arc, I pretended to struggle as the newly fuelled flames licked around the chair legs. The rope did catch fire, and so did the legs of the chair, but because the timing had not been orchestrated by Metro-Goldwyn-Mayer, the rope didn't give way and within a few minutes the flames were spreading to the broken cane seat and licking round the seat of my pants. I tried to move, but realised that if the chair toppled, I would fall headlong into the flames. I had to be hauled from the fire by Mickey, who grabbed the back of the chair just as the broken leg collapsed, but mercifully before my trousers were alight. He beat out the flames with an old curtain that he found in the hedge bottom.

I escaped with nothing more than melted soles on my shoes, and clothing that smelled like a kipper. I might not have got the girl, but like the goody in the film, I had cheated the flames, if not in quite such an heroic fashion.

At any rate, Mickey seemed impressed. I'd never seen him looking so worried. We said goodbye at his garden gate. I thought he looked paler than usual.

I didn't tell my mum what had happened. I said that Mr Hudson had been having a bonfire and that we'd been helping him and that was why my clothes smelled of smoke.

She wasn't impressed. 'Why he has to have so many fires I don't know. He's only got a small garden, and anyway, there's never anything in it.'

I didn't reply. I was happy to have got away with it. It never occurred to me that I'd actually been lucky to get away with my life. But more importantly, Mum never did find out.

I promised myself that I would do two things before I was forty – learn to play the piano and ride a horse. On the first count I failed. I did make an attempt to become a pianist, but after six months of lessons my teacher moved away (she swore it was nothing to do with my progress) and I never got round to enlisting the help of another. Four chords and what my dad used to call: 'Oh, can you wash my father's shirt; oh, can you wash it clean; oh, can you wash my father's shirt and hang it on the line' are my only party pieces. There is not much call for them.

But I did learn to ride, and even jump a little, on a wonderful sixteen-hand grey ex-team chaser called Thistle. I don't ride very often now, but there is little to compare with the thrill of kicking a horse into a gallop at the bottom of a field of stubble and clinging on for dear life with your heels and your head down.

Since being a lad, I've had a love affair with horses – in paint and in the flesh. The works of George Stubbs and Sir Alfred Munnings thrill me like no others. Dogs command affection, cats command attention, but horses command respect.

'Osses

Cars might have been a rarity in our street, but there were plenty of them in the town: luxurious Humbers and modest Standard Eights, Austin Cambridges and Morris Oxfords, sit-up-and-beg Ford Populars and elegant Wolseleys – the only car that had 'its name up in lights', with a little illuminated badge at the top of the radiator grill.

Old Mr Spooner, who looked like Winston Churchill and even smoked a fat cigar, was driven to his little factory at the top of Brewery Road in a black Rolls Royce. He sat in the back, swamped by a big black overcoat with an astrakhan collar, the eyes in his round, white head peering through thick horn-rimmed spectacles. Nobody envied him the car; it just seemed oddly out of place in Ilkley. I mean, why would you want a Rolls Royce just to ride to the top of Brewery Road? You might just as well walk.

My dad, who rode to work on his big black bike with his tool bag balanced on the crossbar, was always desperate for a Rover 90 – like Miss Coffey, the Brown Owl of the local Brownie pack. He never got one. He had to settle, eventually, for an Austin A55 pick-up van, and we all four piled on to the front bench seat. The Mini pick-up that followed resulted in Kath and me being relegated to the back. Miss Coffey lived up Curly Hill and came from a family with private means. As a plumber, Dad's means were more public. But he could dream.

As Miss Coffey cruised by, waving politely from the high driving seat, my father would touch his cap and gaze dreamily in the direction of the thin wisp of blue-grey exhaust until the car purred out of sight. Dad would have loved a car that purred; instead, he ended up with one that grunted.

231

Cars excited me as much as any lad in the 1950s, but the things that made the hairs on the back of my neck stand on end were the horses. There weren't many of them, but those that trotted into my life made a big impression.

At the bottom of Nelson Road is Little Lane. It's more of a road than a lane, really, and destined in a few hundred yards to turn into the more salubrious-sounding Valley Drive – a more suitable name for a road in Ben Rhydding. At its junction with Nelson Road was Little Lane Garage. This wasn't a flashy filling station with illuminated petrol pumps; it was a workaday repair shop with huge sliding doors of green-painted corrugated iron. It was here that the broken-down Standard Eights and old Ford Pops were taken to be mended; the Humbers and the Wolseleys would go to Ross's Garage in Ben Rhydding – the only Rolls Royce dealer for miles around, and the supplier of Mr Spooner's gleaming limousine.

The towering doors of Little Lane Garage were heaved open in the morning and stayed that way until early evening, during which time fountains of sparks from the welding equipment would shower out on to the pavement to the alarm of passers-by, who would skip smartly sideways to avoid lasting damage.

Behind the garage was a small alley. It was unmade and scattered along its sides were assorted lumps of scrap iron and rusting mudguards, old cartwheels and oil drums. They'd been there so long that tall grass grew up between them, and slicks of oily water snaked across the black, compacted earth. If you walked past this cavalcade of cast-offs, side-stepping the slippery slicks, you would come to a large black shed – the blacksmith's forge, where the furnace roared and the bellows belched from dawn till dusk.

Sam Rayner was a big man with a massive leather apron. His face was the colour of pale leather, and his brow would run with sweat. His cap – once tweed – was now the texture of greasy canvas and flattened to his head, and there were black marks round his eyes and smudges on his chin.

I didn't believe that he had feet. His apron was so long and his walk so loping that I was convinced he had hooves, and that they were probably shod with iron shoes like the clogs my mum used to wear when she worked in the mill before she married.

You'd seldom see him standing. He'd almost always be bent double with his back to the rear end of a horse; the hefty hoof pulled up between his legs as he trimmed its edges or hammered in the nails or deftly twisted off the unwanted ends with some evil-looking tool.

His forge was full of tools. They hung from nails on the beams, and lay in great piles on a bench to the side of the furnace. I'd watch with a gormless stare as he fashioned a shoe from raw metal, pulling it yellow-hot from the furnace in the end of a pair of grips, and beating it into a crescent moon on his anvil – one hard stroke on the horseshoe, one soft stroke on the anvil; one hard stroke on the horseshoe, one soft stroke on the anvil; CLANG-clang, CLANG-clang, CLANG-clang – like church bells. In and out of the furnace the shoe would come, until it was shaped to his liking and he'd hold it against the hoof of the horse to see if it was a perfect fit. This was when the foul-smelling mixture of smoke and steam and burning hoof would fill the air, and I'd stuff my snotty hanky over my nose to block it out.

Sam Rayner hardly ever spoke – at least, not to the kids who crowded round his doorway. But he never chased us off; just carried on doing his work until we got bored of watching. The horses came and went, usually without a murmur, but we would flatten ourselves against the side of the shed as they were led away, fearful of a kick in the goolies.

'Them big 'uns can kick so 'ard that yer bollocks 'ud never come down again,' said Dokey Gell. We didn't want to put it to the test.

Riders came from all over the town to have their horses shod at Sam Rayner's, but I never remember seeing Mrs Briggs there. She drove round the town in a horse and buggy, instead of a car, and was a strange sight, among the rest of the traffic. She had what I think was the most serene and delicate face I have ever seen. It was small, like Mrs Briggs herself, rose pink and fine-featured. Her froth of lightly curled hair was silver grey and she wore fragile-looking rimless spectacles and a blissful smile whatever the weather. She was the most unlikely looking pig-keeper I have ever seen, but from time to time, the buggy would be replaced with a more robust wooden-sided cart into which half a dozen swill-filled metal dustbins would be placed. She would ride in this through the town, and despite the fact that she wore old clothes, black wellingtons that seemed far too big for her and a jacket held in place with string, she looked to me, always, like a refugee from *My Fair Lady* – a diminutive Queen of Transylvania who just happened to be dressed in rags. Always she smiled absently as she rode by, untainted by the scent of swill she left in her wake.

At the top of Brook Street, the Times Square of Ilkley, was an elaborate fountain composed of prancing white horses. In the early days it shot plumes of water into the air, and while its equine element never ranked with the horses of St Mark's in Venice, it was, in its own small way, a prominent landmark in the town. Eventually, during the days when it was switched off more often than it was on, someone sneaked out at dead of night and painted it red. It was the beginning of the end, and the fountain and the horses, seen as too great a temptation for vandals, were eventually removed and replaced with an uninspired circular flower bed.

For some unaccountable reason the area around the fountain was known as the Monkey Rack. It might have been a reference to its use as a pick-up point for courting couples. Certainly 'I'll meet you at the Monkey Rack' was a well-used phrase – the spot being the junction between the two main shopping streets – and it was a favourite location for courting couples to canoodle on the benches after dark. It was also the place where I saw a man who was a legend among Yorkshire folk at that time – William Holt.

I heard him before I saw him. 'Whoaaa!' was the cry. It came bellowing out of thin air and nearly lifted me out of my shoes. I was dawdling along, not looking where I was going – Lone Rangering, probably. I turned round and saw directly behind me a towering brown-and-white horse and, on top of it, like St George on his charger, a man with a large moustache, riding boots and breeches and a tweed jacket. There were leather saddlebags on either side of the horse, and having stopped the towering steed in its tracks, the rider slid down off the animal's back and began to unbuckle them.

I didn't know who he was. He looked a bit scary, and I remembered what my mum had said about strange men. They didn't come stranger than this one. I backed off towards the side of the fountain, but peered round it furtively and watched what happened.

Several people crossed the street to greet him. He shook their hands, and boomed his hellos like something out of Charles Dickens. As well as telling me about the dangers of talking to strange men, my mother had also told me about *The Pickwick Papers*. Here was Mr Pickwick to the life.

He dipped into one of the saddlebags and pulled out a handful of books. He began to sign them and handed them out to the people around him. 'That'll be fifteen shillings.' They'd give him a pound note and he'd pull change from the other saddlebag. The whole procedure was over within ten minutes, then he was back on the horse and away. It was only later, after he'd ridden off, quite literally, into the sunset, that I discovered who he was. A man with a small boy had bought one of his books – *The Wizard of Whirlaw*. He showed me what it said on the dust jacket.

William Holt started work as a weaver at the age of twelve and at the same time taught himself four languages, writing the words in the dust on the beams above his loom. Then he began to travel. He sailed up the Yangtze, and travelled to America and Japan, Russia and Persia. He boasted that he had 'sailed through the Yellow Sea with a murderer, struggled with a madman armed with a fire-axe onboard a ship in a typhoon, was challenged to a duel in Seville and almost murdered in Japan'.

He built his own sailing ship while working in logging camps on the Pacific Coast of Canada, and reported from the Spanish Civil War. Then he founded British Mobile Libraries and Books on Wheels, before going on to invent and patent an improved shuttle for automatic looms.

The Wizard of Whirlaw was the third book he had published 'off his own bat' and he rode around Yorkshire on his horse, selling it from his saddlebag.

Last year I found a copy in a second-hand bookshop, and forty-five years after seeing the author flogging it for fifteen bob, I bought it for £6.89. It is a curious read; a bit dated and full of 'messages', but the plaudits on the back of the dust jacket are those that any writer would be proud of. Along with encouraging quotes of Holt's work from *The Times Literary Supplement*, and the *Daily Dispatch*, are the endorsements of two notable names: 'I recommend it highly as a bedside book', H. G. Wells; and 'Mr Holt's autobiography is of a kind rather more unusual nowadays', George Orwell.

You can't argue with Orwell. Unusual is definitely the right word. I looked up in time to see William Holt, author, adventurer, explorer, war correspondent, linguist and inventor of the automatic shuttle trotting off down Brook Street and shouting a greeting to Mrs Briggs, who was trotting upwards on the other side with her dustbins full of pigswill. Her eyes sparkled more than usual as she shot him a melting smile and gave a gentle wave.

I've had the greatest respect for horsemen and women ever since.

Like all the lads in our street, I couldn't wait to drive, but when you're eight or nine, seventeen seems light years away. There were no Chopper bikes or skateboards in the 1950s – you had either a second-hand bike from the saleroom or a Palm Beach from the Wharfedale Cycle Depot on Leeds Road. If you were happy to pay on the never-never, there was Mrs Woodrup's catalogue, or if you had patience and a couple of stressed-out parents, there were Kensitas cigarette gift coupons.

But with a bit of ingenuity and some old pram wheels, we could each make our own customised form of transport. They varied in horsepower, safety features and design, but they all provided one thing – the ability to travel faster than walking pace down the middle of Nelson Road.

Wheels

'What the bloody 'ell's that?' asked Stuart Whittaker.
He was older than I was, and always a bit dismissive. I think he thought there was something deeply suspicious about a lad who liked gardening. That's probably why he called me 'Petunia'. I think the other kids in the street thought he meant to say 'Petula'. They knew who Petula Clark was, but petunia was not part of their vocabulary.

Stuart's incredulity on this particular day was not directed at my gardening, but at my transport.

Before we all had bikes, there were other, more spectacular ways of getting about. Almost without exception, every kid in the street had a bogie – a wooden cart on wheels, on which you could lie down and propel yourself from the top of the street to the bottom; steering with a piece of rope attached to the front axle.

Some bogies had large wheels, some had small wheels, usually nicked from prams and pushchairs that had fallen apart.

Mickey Hudson's was made from one of his dad's orange boxes and so was always a bit fragile. The wheels were small, too, and felt every bump down the road. Every time he rode it, Mickey would get off looking mildly concussed. Stephen Feather – Fezz to his mates – had one that was the bottom of a pram, big, curly springs included. Fezz's dad was never much of a one for DIY, and so Fezz sat on a plank tied between the axles. He'd shoot down the road like Boadicea in her chariot, and woe betide you if your shins got in the way. Fezz's springs could inflict damage every bit as severe as Boadicea's knives.

I was rather proud of my bogie, built in the cellar by my dad, from two pairs of large pram wheels and three floorboards, and fitted with a brake – a lump of wood that was pivoted so it could be brought into contact with one of the back wheels. Used insensitively, the effect of the brake would be sudden and quite dramatic – the vehicle spinning round and hurling the occupant into the road. Gravel burns were frequent.

On the particular day that Stuart Whittaker saw me, I had converted my bogie into a chuck wagon. An old blackout curtain had been fastened over four lumps of broom handle that were used as uprights, and I'd made cardboard AA and RAC signs for the front, plus a tax disc – the sort of optional extras that were all the rage in the Wild West.

With much more wind resistance, I discovered that I could push off the bogie at the top of the street and sit there with my hands on the reins while it chugged slowly downhill, hardly touching the brake. The ride was not as thrilling, admittedly, but it would last longer, and with no need to apply the brake, the bogie would just grind to a halt at the bottom of the road. That way, the chances of gravel burns or warning toots from Samuel Ledgard's buses were more unlikely. I was happy.

'Yer daft bugger! Why don't you go any faster? Chicken!' Stuart would shout after me. I'd bite my lip and pretend I didn't care.

And anyway, the chuck-wagon mode wouldn't last long. Soon

I'd tire of the slow speed and decide that it was, indeed, a racing car that I needed. The blackout material would go back into the house, the AA and RAC signs into the dustbin, and my sleek new machine – with silver sticky tape from the bike shop stuck down the side for go-faster stripes – would become a souped-up motor.

I'd lie down head first on the wooden boards and shorten the steering rope. Then I'd kick off at the top of Nelson Road and career down to the bottom, teeth clenched, praying all the while that I would not encounter Mrs Barker with her shopping – 'Get off the pavement, you silly boy!' – that a bus would not come out of the garage and that no traffic would be crossing Little Lane when I shot across it and down the blacksmith's track.

Most of the time I got away with it. Now and again I came to grief. If a bus did decide to come out of the garage, I would have to bring kamikaze techniques into play – throwing myself off the bogie and allowing it to crash into the bus-garage wall with great risk of damage.

One day, while my mum was out shopping, Mickey Hudson, employing just these sort of tactics, saw his bogie shoot underneath the bus, as he rolled clear. Off down the road went Samuel Ledgard's blue double-decker, and somewhere underneath it, embedded in its exhaust system, went Mickey's bogie, too. They never found it. At least, not while we were around to blame.

My dad had made my bogie well. The nuts and bolts that held on the metal axles lasted for several weeks, but finally metal fatigue got the better of even them.

'Can you mend it?' I'd ask.

'I've done it twice. Why don't you do it yourself?'

His impatience was understandable. There were enough jobs to do around the house without continually having to repair my wheels.

I searched around in the cellar and found a hammer and some nails. My skills did not extend to the use of a screwdriver. The axle would be lined up, the nails bashed into the rough lump of wood, and then bent over to hold the metal rod in place. I would get another half-dozen runs out of the bogie until the nails fell out. Then the axle would part from the body once more and the bogie would thud to a halt, to be overtaken by the wheels making their bid for freedom down the hill.

In moments of supreme independence I would take the bogie up to the moors. The trouble was, it didn't run nearly so well on the rough tracks that wove between bracken and heather, though I could career over a really steep bank of heather and down the rocky slopes of Backstone Beck, landing up in the water and then traipsing back home with squelching socks. If the water in the river was cold, then the water in the moorland stream was icy.

Once a week, on a Saturday morning, my bogie would be commandeered by Dad. 'They're not clean trousers, are they?' he'd enquire, doing up the fastenings on his bib-and-brace overalls.

'No. I've worn them all week.'

'That's all right, then. Come on.'

Dad would walk, while I lay on a rough hessian sack on the bogie and pushed it with one leg, along Little Lane and down Lower Wellington Road to the gasworks.

' 'Ello, 'Arry. 'Alf a 'undredweight of number three, please,' my dad would bellow above the din.

Harry Thwaites, on duty there every Saturday morning, his face blackened from the coke dust, would take the sack and hold it under an enormous steel hopper. Happy that it was secure, he'd then pull a lever and the coke would thunder out of the hopper into the sack. The trick was to stop the flow when there was just enough slack left at the top of the bag to allow a lump of sisal twine to be fastened round it. Too full and Harry would curse and pull some of the coke out with his horny, calloused hands that were by now the same colour as the coke; too empty and my dad would raise an eyebrow at being given short measure.

The half-crown having been handed over, the plump and dusty sack would be flung on to the bogie and with Dad on the rope at the front, and me with my back to the heavy load and pushing with my legs, we'd make the slower return journey uphill.

Once home, Dad would lift the sack from the bogie, untie the string, and tip the contents down the coal chute into the cellar. The sack would be rolled up, the string tied round it, and the neat package put on a shelf in the cellar until next week's trip.

Until then I'd be free to use the bogie as I wished: to race the other lads in the street, to take it down to the riverside gardens where smooth tarmac paths criss-crossed the grass, or, as on one particularly eventful day, to intercept my mum at the bottom of the street and load up the bogie with her shopping.

'That's very nice. Have you had a good morning?'

'Yeah. All right.'

'Anything exciting?'

'Not really.' I didn't tell her about Mickey's bogie going underneath the bus. After careful consideration I didn't think it was a good idea.

The litany of stations from Ilkley to Leeds is as vivid to me today as it was then: Ilkley, Ben Rhydding, Burley in Wharfedale, Menston, Guiseley, Rawdon, Newlay and Horsforth, Calverley and Rodley, Kirkstall and Leeds City. There was always a sigh of relief when we tumbled off the train back in Ilkley, walking out under the big-faced clock on the end wall of the station, weary and coated in city grime, to walk along Railway Road and Trafalgar Road, back to number 34 Nelson Road, where the kettle would be put on, the fire lit, and my sister and I would climb the stairs to our bedrooms to play with whatever we'd been bought to keep us quiet while Mum tried on the hat or Dad the suit.

It wouldn't be much. An Airfix kit of a Spitfire for me, and a cut-out doll with dresses for Kath. I'd hare up to my bedroom at the top of the house — a converted attic — and look out through the dormer window at the moors, happy to be home and away from the clamour of the city.

Only once a year did Ilkley succumb to rampant commercialism, and then it had a kind of glamour all its own.

The Trades Fair

Once a year, in the King's Hall and Winter Gardens – Ilkley's Edwardian assembly rooms – the local shopkeepers got together, courtesy of the local Chamber of Trade, and put on the Trades Fair. To London children accustomed to bright lights and hoopla, it would have been a tame affair, but for the kids in this small northern town, it was the glamorous event of the year. Entry was free, and for as long as you wanted you could wander around between washing machines and fridges, bicycles and motor scooters lit up like movie stars and pirouetting on revolving turntables to the strains of piped music. There would be wardrobes with ornamental gadroons on the doors made by Maurice Booth, Ilkley's finest cabinet-maker, and electric train layouts built by Mr Marshall – the man with the sweet shop that also sold toys.

'I'll meet you there at six o'clock,' said Mickey Hudson, and as the town-hall clock struck the hour, we sauntered in, hands in pockets, to see what we could get for nothing.

On the stage of the King's Hall, the Gas Board would have several kitchens laid out with the latest labour-saving appliances – an eye-level grill or a glass-doored oven – and there would be leaflets, hundreds of them, to be collected and put in a carrier bag for inspection that evening when you got home. It didn't matter what they were; it was enough to have them.

Collecting things was something we all felt driven to do; there was some kind of security in ownership of a collection, some kind of status. In leaner weeks we'd search through the dustbins at the back of the bus garage at the bottom of the street when the drivers and conductors were at work, picking out from among the fag ends and sweet packets the ends of bus-ticket rolls – discarded once the central pink line appeared to show that there were only several feet of paper left. We'd pull out cigarette packets and tear off the front and back covers so that each became a crude playing card. With these we'd play snap, and feel as rich as a king when we scooped a whole pile of them.

There were the cheap brands that were not much treasured – the green-and-orange Woodbine packet, the creamy-coloured Player's Weights, the nautical Player's Navy Cut, with the picture of the bearded sailor, and the sober Senior Service packet in white and navy blue. Most of them were from packets of ten, but sometimes there were twenties of classy fags like Olivier and du Maurier that were prized far beyond their actual worth.

After the Trades Fair, we could boast of far grander pieces of paper and cardboard showing illustrations of the latest record player or wireless, or the bike that everybody wanted but nobody would ever have.

Parents came to check out a new bed, or to look at the light fittings that hung from temporary ceilings erected by Arthur English on the Grove, but for Mickey and me, once we'd watched Mr Marshall's trains go round the track a couple of times, and asked for anything with Hornby Dublo or Tri-ang printed on it, there were just two shops that cut the mustard – Allen and Walker, the record shop, and Mr Oliver, the nurseryman.

Long before Woolworths started selling records, Allen and Walker at the bottom of Cowpasture Road had built two sound booths lined with pegboard where you could go and shut yourself in while they played you the single of your choice. At four shillings and sixpence they were not cheap, and it seemed only a matter of months before these products of Parlophone and Columbia were six shillings and fourpence.

With a shilling pocket money a week, it would be a month or more before you could afford to buy one, but then to have the latest single before anybody else did was the kind of one-upmanship we all aspired to. I was the first kid in our street to own 'She Loves You', but long before that I had invested in Russ Conway's 'China Tea' and discovered the hard way that it had much less in the way of social cachet.

On their stand in the King's Hall, Allen and Walker would show off the very latest in Fidelity record players and appropriately named Wharfedale speakers. It was here that Dad bought his classical selections, but Mickey and I had different tastes back then.

'Have you got any Elvis Presley?'

'Course we' ave,' replied the assistant.

'Can you put it on?' asked Mickey.

'No. They won't let me. You've got to listen to this stuff.' He pointed upwards into the air, indicating the sickly strains of Mantovani and 'Charmaine', which was supposedly more conducive to selling fridges and cookers.

'They might enjoy it.'

'So would I, but I'd lose me job.'

Sometimes I'd go to the Trades Fair on my own, sometimes with a mate, and sometimes with Mum and Dad, though progress with them tended to be rather slow, and they'd stop and look at things that bored me rigid, like bedroom furniture and three-piece suites in uncut moquette, whatever that was, from Darbysons of Burley.

I don't recall Mum and Dad ever buying anything from the Trades Fair, except the records, but it gave them ideas. Mum would scrutinise the new washing machines, and Dad would talk knowledgeably to the proprietor, and the following day she'd be in the library looking up *Which?* to see what they recommended.

Her curiosity satisfied and her sense of values placated, we'd go home again and wait until Mrs Woodrup dropped off her fat mail-order catalogue. If the item was small – a record player or a wireless – we'd get it from her with monthly payments, though even these small ventures into HP frightened my mum. She'd far rather pay for everything when she had it, rather than get it on the never-never. To her the phrase 'Frees you from pre-set spending limits' was another way of saying 'Allows you to live beyond your means'.

Every Friday, when Dad came home with his wages, he'd hand them over to Mum, who would sit down and do her accounts with a series of little cash boxes from Woolworths. The insurance man, the milkman, the electricity and the gas were all accounted for, then there would be the lump for housekeeping and, finally, Dad's pocket money for his nights out at the Station Hotel playing dominoes with 'the lads'.

My own pocket money amounted to one shilling. It never changed for years, it seemed. It didn't buy much, but most of it went in Woolworths on seeds, or 'construction kits', though at the Trades Fair there was another temptation – Mr Oliver's nursery stand.

The small nursery along Springs Lane, opposite the Coronation Hospital, was not somewhere I went regularly. It was up the other end of town from us. But at the Trades Fair, Mr Oliver really went to town. His stand would be full of house plants – weeping figs and rubber plants, ferns and gardenias – things of such exotic origins that I'd never think of owning them.

The urge I had to own a rubber plant was all-consuming. I'd swotted up on its Latin name – an easy one to remember – *Ficus elastica*. But rubber plants were five shillings – more than a month's pocket money. Even a record was cheaper, and it gave me more prestige among the other kids in the street.

I inspected the dozen or more rubber plants on Mr Oliver's stand with a covetous eye.

'D'ya want one, then?' he asked. He was a wiry man with iron-grey hair and olive-coloured skin.

'Yes. But I can't afford one.'

'Why d'ya like 'em?'

'I like the leaves. I like the way they're all waxy. And that red thing coming out of the top.'

'That's the new leaf – all rolled up and waiting to uncurl.'

'Mmm.'

I knew it was no good. I could look at those rubber plants until the cows came home, but I couldn't afford one. Mr Oliver saw my predicament.

'I'll tell you what . . .' he said. 'Have some of these.' He reached up to a beam, from which hung different kinds of leaves, tied into bundles for flower arrangers. He pulled down a cluster of deep-purple, glossy ones.

I took them from him and turned them over in my hand. They were amazing – shiny as steel but soft as supple leather. 'What are they?'

'Magnolia leaves; they've been treated with wax. They'll last for ages.'

I thanked him, probably less effusively than I should have done on account of being lost in wonder and also overwhelmed by his generosity. The magnolia leaves were probably only worth a few pence, but they were things of such incomparable natural beauty and simplicity that they took my breath away.

I took them home and kept them in a drawer in my bedroom – to be taken out and stroked from time to time, held up to the light and admired. Mr Oliver was not wrong. They lasted for several years before they finally fell apart, but the thrill of owning them is with me still, and they fuelled a passion that seemed to increase almost daily. A passion for things that grow.

I think I'd have swapped anything up to the age of fifteen for a bit of height. I was, as befitted the first part of my surname, small. Four feet ten in the fourth form, rising to five feet one by the time I left school at fifteen. I've claimed five feet nine since I was eighteen, but according to the tape measure, I've been lying. I'm five feet eight and a half inches. Maybe I've started shrinking.

Moving On Up

T he fact that I failed my eleven-plus came as no surprise to anybody, least of all me. There was, for a moment or two, a faint glimmer of hope, I suppose. A brief flash of optimism when I mused on the fact that I might know the answers to some of the questions on the sheets of paper in front of me and be capable of expressing myself. But they didn't last long. They went out of the window the moment I saw John Brown was still writing long after I had finished, and that he was on about his third page. Still, I hadn't made too many blots on the one I had completed.

I don't remember the moment when I heard I was one of those who would be going to the secondary rather than the grammar, but it can't have come as a shock. There would have been that momentary stab of regret at another failure, but then, when I had taken the trouble to consider the sort of mental struggle that grammar school would have posed for the next six years – among all those 'brainy' girls and boys – I knew that I had been put in the right place. Funny how ridiculous that sounds now – brainy. But that's what we called them then, the bright kids. The ones who grasped concepts readily, instead of sitting there with a furrowed brow trying to make sense of the teacher's complicated ramblings. I can recall that feeling now – the feeling of trying to knit fog. I caught up in the years that followed, but at the age of eleven it is no consolation to know that you are a late developer. Who's to say whether you'll develop at all? And into what?

'Anyway, the uniform is nicer,' my mother offered by way of consolation. There was no disappointment on her part, just resignation. She knew all along that her little boy was not really cut out for an academic life. 'Bright but not brainy,' she'd say. It was probably a bit of a relief. The mention of the uniform would be her way of moving things on. The secondary-school uniform was a navy-blue blazer with a navy- and royal-blue tie and grey shorts. Until you got to the fourth form – then you could wear long trousers. The grammar-school pupils wore striped blazers of bottle green, silver and black – like something from Henley Royal Regatta – and they got told off if they didn't wear their caps. Our caps were optional, or at least they seemed to be. Most of us wore them simply to keep warm. The winters were bitter back then. Come the spring, though, they'd be consigned to the bottom of the wardrobe, along with the garters that were used to hold up our socks, and the stiffeners from our shirt collars. Socks round the ankles, capless heads and curly collars were the signs of a second-former, but first-formers were started off as their mothers hoped they meant to go on – smartly attired in full uniform. There was method in this: it meant that the rest of your clothes got less wear and tear.

So off we poled, down to the Co-op, interrupting Mr Hay's lunch yet again, as he came through the mirrored swing door finishing off his sandwich.

He eyed me up and occasionally measured things with the tape that hung round his neck, then laid everything out on the wooden counter – the vests and the underpants, the socks and the shirts, the tie and the blazer and the cap. Everything except the shorts. He hadn't any small enough, so Mum had to make those on her sewing machine.

'That's a bit of a dint in my housekeeping, Mr Hay,' she muttered.

Mr Hay smiled weakly, but offered no discount. 'At least you'll get your divi,' he consoled.

'Go on, then, wrap them up.'

'What number?'

'One seven two nine seven three,' Mum intoned. It was a number we used every week at the Co-op butcher's where the massive Mr Hogg, whose hands were like bunches of sausages, weighed our meat on his hefty white Avery scales. Never was a man more aptly named.

256

We never used the Co-op grocer's in between Mr Hay's drapery and Mr Hogg's butchery. The stuff there was 'a bit cheap', said Mum, by which she meant inferior rather than economical. For groceries we went to Mr Elwood down Leeds Road, who would deliver the order in a cardboard box once a week – with a packet of Spangles each as a treat for me and Kath, and the packet of washing-up powder wrapped in newspaper so that it didn't taint the food.

But Mr Hay and Mr Hogg had passed muster, and the Co-op divi came in handy at Christmas when it could be traded in for seasonal treats – a lump of boiled ham or a bit of sirloin. Mum would get a fair bit bearing in mind the clothes we had just bought.

'What about a satchel?' Mr Hay enquired.

'Oh, I hadn't thought about that.' My mother looked worried.

He brought one out for her to look at. It was too expensive.

'Real leather, mind,' Mr Hay reassured her.

'Yes, I'm sure. But have you anything more reasonable?' It was never 'cheaper', always 'more reasonable'.

We looked at a briefcase, but it was decided that it was too grown-up and still a bit pricey. We settled in the end on a small fibreboard suitcase that was painted brown to look like leather.

'Yes, that'll do,' said Mum, having had me walk up and down the shop holding it in my hand to see if it looked right.

With me hanging on to my newly acquired luggage, and Mum cradling the brown paper parcel of clothes, we walked up the street back home for a consoling plate of Mr Hogg's sausages and a dollop of mashed potato.

I spent the first term of my secondary-school life in a large house at the top of a street just off the Grove. 'One Oak' was an old Victorian villa that had been pressed into service for the first-formers until the brand-new school on Valley Drive was ready just after Christmas. The rooms of One Oak were lofty and echoing, and there wasn't much in the way of a playground except the small tarmac drive at the front of the house below the tree that gave it its name.

Here, I had my first taste of homework, of the art of Picasso and van Gogh, and of the cane – three swipes across the bum for sheltering in the porch when it was raining; the teacher said it wasn't – spitting did not constitute light drizzle.

At least they didn't call me 'Titty' at secondary school. That name had already been foisted on my cousin David. I got 'Titchy' from the girls and 'Fred' from the boys – the first a cute sympathy vote, and the second a mickey-take of my then unfashionable middle name.

After Christmas we moved to the brand-new school on Valley Drive, with a hall and a stage, a proper art room, a library and a laboratory complete with gas taps and sinks.

I tried to excel, and I did enjoy English, even if Miss Weatherall could be discouraging on occasion: 'This is *not* the way to spell "experience"; how many times do I have to tell you?' written in red ink at the bottom of my essay. I thought 'expierience' was a much better spelling.

But for all her discouragement, something in Miss Weatherall's teaching must have ignited a flame. It was probably no more than the merest flicker back then – a dim glow or a tiny spark, barely visible in the darkness of my general ignorance. But she did, somehow, manage to foster an interest in words and convey to me their inherent power. She probably deserves more credit than I have ever given her (but I bet she never thought I'd write for a living).

I managed a B plus at art, thanks to the kindly Miss Gill, who opened my eyes to the work of Augustus John and a woman's cleavage, but not necessarily in that order, and later Mr Wildman, who encouraged me in drama. My French accent, said Madame Hawksworth, was, if anything, a little too strong. What a shame that my written work did not demonstrate the same enthusiasm. 'When it comes to writing about the weather "It is *pleuting*" might be amusing, but "*Il pleut*" would be more correct.'

I should have been better at science, bearing in mind my future, but Miss Sutcliffe – known as 'the Improper Fraction' (top-heavy) – was a loud woman who frightened the life out of me. When she bawled at you, 'Acids must be respected!' you felt obliged to scatter the vinegar on to your fish and chips with particular care.

I was good with my hands so it seemed perverse that I could not attend rural studies and woodwork classes, but these were reserved for the B, C and D classes, not the A stream in which I found myself. So there must have been some glimmer of intelligence visible to my teachers even then. Perhaps they thought that patience might pay off.

I just wished I could grow a bit. I was cannon fodder for any ambitious school bully. The bitter irony of not being allowed to do woodwork was brought home to me one day when one of the B stream worked his way round the playground with a lump of knotted seagrass – the stuff from which they make the seats for Shaker chairs and stools. He'd walk up behind any suitable victim wearing shorts and flick it at the backs of their legs. It stung like hell.

I am a placid sort, not given to violence or loss of temper on a regular basis, but when it snaps, it snaps. My knees shake and I find myself in possession of far more bravery than is probably wise in a person of modest physical attributes.

He came up behind me, and the first I knew of it was the stinging sensation at the back of my knees. I leaped forward. So did he, and started to whip me around the playground like a pony being broken in. I stood it for about three strokes of the lash, then I turned round and stared him in the face. Well, I stared up at where his face would be – he was taller than I was, and broader, too. The fact that I had stopped must have deprived him, momentarily, of his impetus. In that split second, I snatched the seagrass from his hand and pro-ceeded to dispense the same treatment to the back of *his* legs. He jumped back once, then twice. Before he had a chance to jump a third time, or, more likely, to regain his composure and grab the seagrass back, I threw it in his face and marched away, convinced that he would follow and do me untold damage. He didn't. Instead, he slunk off in the direction of his girlfriend, who had been watching the whole thing from the sidelines.

I had always fancied her. She was the most beautiful girl in our class, with long, blonde hair and a clear complexion. I managed to get a snog with her behind a curtain at one of the class Christmas parties that Dorothy Robinson organised in the Congregational hall, but she did not seem keen to prolong the relationship and soon moved on to another windowsill. Then she took up with the bully and I kept my distance.

I watched him walk over to her. She glanced in my direction. I like to think that I gave a good account of myself in her eyes. But whatever she really thought, she never came my way again. But then, neither did he.

I did not make any staunch friends at school. I suppose I should feel embarrassed to admit as much, but I can't. There was never anybody I felt completely at ease with or whom I completely trusted, and I envy those folk who are still close to their school friends later in life. I've never really analysed why it happened this way. I don't think it was a personal deficiency or any particular reflection on my classmates. Maybe I just wasn't ready to commit back then. My closest friends are those I made in my early twenties, and thirty-odd years on we remain as comfortable in each other's company and even more at ease with our respective foibles than we did back then. It was worth the wait.

The Lame Duck

I 'd not really taken much notice of Keith. He'd been in 2B and
that meant he might just as well have been in another country.
It's not that those of us in 2A regarded ourselves as being acade-
mically superior (well, not that much); it's just that you couldn't
really get to know someone well over the space of two playtimes and
a school dinner. Not in the same way that you could if you spent
every waking moment from nine till four sitting with them and their
wind problems in the airless confines of a classroom.

I'd notice him across the playground sometimes. Standing on his
own, or trying with an assumed bravado to involve himself in
some game that the others were playing. It never worked, and
he'd scuttle off again, with expletives ringing in his ears, trying to
look as though it didn't really matter, and bouncing his body
against the chain-link fencing in the repetitive fashion of the
terminally bored.

Keith was one of those lads who'd been dealt a duff hand by
nature. He had a withered arm and one leg slightly shorter than the
other, which gave him a lopsided walk. His head was an odd shape.
It wasn't exactly deformed, but it wasn't regular either, and his teeth
were too big for his mouth. His hair had been cut by someone who
was clearly a stranger to scissors.

He wore glasses, and while none of the bespectacled lads in my
class had what today we'd call 'designer frames', Keith's were more
old-fashioned than anybody else's. The thick horn-rimmed type that
dads and uncles wore.

I never expected to know him at all. True enough, I was a bit of a
loner myself, being small and not regarded as 'one of the gang' at

school, but I still had my pride, and Keith was obviously way below me.

Then one day he fell across my path. Or was knocked into it. I was walking to school along Valley Drive, having forgotten my bus fare for the umpteenth time, when a lumpen body bounced on to the pavement in front of me. It was Keith.

It all happened so fast. I remember him writhing around on the floor, and shouting, 'Ooh, sir! Sir!'

It was an odd sort of thing to shout. And then I saw what, or rather who, he was shouting at. It was the driver of a Bedford van, who was leaping down from his cab, his face twisted with worry. He'd clipped Keith as he'd been crossing the road.

I'd no doubt that it had been Keith's fault. Everything was Keith's fault. The van driver thought so, and so did Keith, which explained his agonised apology. 'Ooh, sir! I'm so sorry.'

Where others would have cursed and railed at the motor that had just run them down, Keith's natural and instinctive reaction was to apologise for being in the wrong place at the wrong time.

The driver, having checked that no bones were broken, and that he was unlikely to be sued, straightened himself up and said, 'Daft bugger!' Then he hauled himself back into his cab and drove off, drowning the two of us in a cloud of blue exhaust.

'Oh, dear!' wailed Keith, trying to get to his feet and failing. I gave him an arm and helped him up. It was difficult to work out whether he was more lopsided than normal. He brushed a tear from his cheek with the back of his dusty hand, and bent down again to retrieve his glasses from the gutter. Sometimes fate is unkind. The glasses were in perfect condition. He put them on, pushed back the lank of hair that had fallen across his face and said, 'I'm sorry.'

'No bother,' I said, trying to sound as though this happened to me every time I walked to school.

Keith's home was in a small cluster of houses high up on the side of the moor. He was ferried to school every day, with the half-dozen other kids from the tiny hamlet, in a maroon minibus driven by a gloomy moustached driver who never spoke. In bitter winters they would often be cut off for days by snowdrifts and never make the journey to school. I envied him that. I could get there in all weathers on foot, on the bus or, in later years, on my bike. I asked him what he was doing walking.

'Wanted to walk the last bit,' he said. 'That's all.' He volunteered no more. Then said, brightly, 'I'm Keith. Keith Ackroyd. I come from Langbar.'

'I know.' I nodded, then glanced at my watch, anxious not to be late and earn yet another detention. 'Want to carry on walking?'

He nodded, and after brushing the dust off his navy-blue school blazer, he limped along beside me, his satchel bouncing off his hip, and the knot of his tie somewhere under his left ear.

It was hard not to feel a stab of sympathy for him, and a wave of guilt swept over me. Guilt at not being nicer to him before, at not making conversation with him in the playground and at watching from a distance as he was ostracised by just about everybody.

Over the next few days I made a point of seeking him out at playtime. He wasn't difficult to find. He would be standing in a corner, examining the contents of his pockets, and trying to look as if he didn't mind being on his own.

But whenever I approached, his eyes lit up and he would show me something he'd found, or collected. Conkers or a foreign coin that 'might be worth loads' or mostly stamps.

He talked about his mother quite a lot, and his younger brother, Davey, who was brighter than he was and went to the grammar school. The stamps were for him. He had a sister, too, Cathy, who was still at All Saints Junior.

Mrs Ackroyd was usually ill, and seemed often to take to her bed. There was no mention of his father. He talked of his mother with a sympathetic fondness that built up a clear picture of her in my mind. She became Dora in *David Copperfield*. A beautiful, waif-like creature who would love to be stronger and look after her children like a mother should, but who succumbed to everything going.

I could see her in my mind's eye, lying back in bed, her fair hair spread fan-like across the pillow, and her pale face pricked with pink at the cheeks as she murmured instructions to Keith about what he should make them all for tea.

The sympathy built, but every so often I felt myself giving in to the attitudes of the other kids. At moments like these I was less of a friend to Keith than I should have been, when they imitated his ungainly walk or poked fun at his slurring speech, thanks to the teeth that were too big for his mouth. I didn't join in with them, but my failure to more openly take his side left me feeling weak and ashamed.

Then, one day, he asked me to go back home with him for tea. I was unsure about the idea. What if his mum was too ill? But he assured me that she was fine. She'd not been very well over the last few weeks, but she was on the mend now and up and about.

I told my mum that I would be late home.

'Where are you going?'

'To Langbar, with Keith.'

'Do we know him?'

'No. I don't think so. He's the one with the limp.'

'In the minibus?'

'Yes.'

'How will you get back?'

'Keith says the milkman will drop me back in town.'

'Well, don't be late. Be back by six, all right?'

I was surprised that I got away with it so lightly. Mum must have had her mind on other things.

That evening I climbed into the minibus with the other half-dozen kids and the man with the moustache who never said anything. He grunted as I clambered on board; there was no further communication for the entire journey.

The lumbering vehicle wheezed its way up the road out of town and climbed towards the distant moors. Now there were no sounds other than the doleful bleating of sheep. Houses gave way to green fields, and green fields to purple moors and drystone walls with the occasional stone cottage clinging to the side of hills thick with heather and bracken. The driver dropped off his passengers one by one, until Keith and I were the only two left. Eventually he pulled up smartly at the end of a row of stone cottages that crouched low against the moorland cairn. He slid open the door. No words, just a tilt of his head to indicate that we should vacate his premises.

As we stepped down on to the gravelly track, so he lumbered off into the distance, the sound of his engine drowned by the mocking cries of blackface sheep.

'Come on, then.' Keith nodded towards the open gate of the garden. Well, it wasn't a garden, really; just an enclosed area of rough grass with a gate that had collapsed against its supporting wall years ago.

He led me down the stony path at the side of the cottage and pushed open the peeling green door that led into the kitchen.

'Hello, Mum! We're home!'

Sitting at the kitchen table, with a cigarette in one hand and her head resting in the other, was a lady with a twisted face, whose hair was scraped back into a greying bun. She looked up.

'Well, put the kettle on, then.' She didn't smile. 'And ask your friend if he'd like a biscuit.' She drew on her cigarette and glanced wistfully out of the window. Her expression was that of someone who had a permanent headache. She seemed to be continuously scowling. Not like Dora at all. It was hard not to feel disappointed. I'd had such a clear picture of this elegant and fragile woman. And she wasn't elegant at all. Just ordinary. And not remotely pretty.

I glanced at Keith. He was beaming from ear to ear and filling the kettle at the single tap that towered over the kitchen sink.

'Alan's come to look at Davey's stamps,' he said.

I tried to look casual. Relaxed even.

'Oh. Waste of time,' she said. That was all.

I sat for what seemed like an age, while Keith made his mother a cup of tea and put it in front of her. She never said thank you. Never met our eyes.

'Come through here,' he said, having completed his catering duties. It was as if his mother's mood washed right over him. His face was bright and he seemed happy to be home.

We walked out of the kitchen through a darkened hallway and into the front room. There was a greying sofa pulled up close to an unlit fire, and in front of the net-curtained window a large square table with a checked cloth laid over it. Bent over several open albums, of the kind sold by Woolworths, and surrounded by envelopes that spilled out stamps of all nations from Abyssinia to Zululand was a ruddy-faced boy with a glint in his eye. He was not at all like Keith. He was good-looking and athletic, and leaned over towards me and shook my hand, eyes sparkling, a beaming smile on his face.

'Hello,' he said expectantly.

'Hi.' Shyness began to take hold. I wished I hadn't come. I saw his grammar-school blazer on the back of his chair, and his cap stuffed into his satchel that lay on the floor.

'Alan's come to look at your stamps.'

I nodded, feebly. I had an album of my own back home. Once, I had tried to work up some kind of enthusiasm for philately. Along with ornithology, it was the only big word I knew. The main attraction of stamps was that you could buy a lot of very colourful ones for very little money, and the fact that you stuck them in albums in rows appealed to my orderly nature. But my heart had never been in it, as a result of which I had a large tin full of stamps and an album full of empty pages.

'Hello,' murmured a small voice from the corner.

I turned round to see a small, fair-haired girl with a length of blanket in her hand. She was sucking one corner. She sat curled up on the sofa, and neither moved nor said anything more for my entire visit.

I leaned over the table and looked at the stamps.

'Great, aren't they?' said Keith. 'Davey's got hundreds of them, haven't you, Davey?'

Davey nodded. 'This one's a good one. It's a Penny Red. Not as valuable as a Penny Black, but it looks the same. Apart from the colour.'

It was my turn to nod. Sagely.

'You like stamps, don't you, Alan?' asked Keith, clearly trying to demonstrate to his brother that we had something in common.

'Yes. Yes, I do.'

'Do you collect them as well?'

'Yes. Well, sort of. I've had them for ages.'

There was the sound of movement outside the door, and Mrs Ackroyd came through from the kitchen.

She took a slurp of her tea and looked critically at the table and its mountain of stamps. 'Another craze.'

'No it's not,' murmured Davey.

'It won't last. What was it last time? Dinky toys?'

Davey looked crestfallen.

Keith tried to pour oil on the troubled waters. 'Alan collects stamps,' he said, hoping, I suppose, to find reinforcements.

'Do you?'

'Yes,' I said, anxious not to let Keith down.

'Well, why don't you give them to him, then?' asked Mrs Ackroyd, ' 'Stead of wasting your time on another craze.'

'It's not a craze,' replied Davey, biting his lip.

'Course it is.' Mrs Ackroyd's face twisted into a weary and disapproving expression.

Keith, anxious now to please both his mother and his guest, said the words that I really wished he hadn't.

'Yes, go on, Davey – do like Mum says. Give them to Alan. He collects stamps. He's really interested.'

I wanted so badly to say that no, I wasn't really, and that Davey should be allowed to keep his stamps. But I couldn't, and I didn't. For reasons of cowardice and of misplaced loyalty, the words would not come. Instead, I saw Davey's look of disappointment as his mother and brother ganged up against him. I saw Keith's lopsided expression as he tried to repay my kindness and placate his mother at one and the same time.

And I saw myself in a new light. That of a false friend who should have known better.

I cannot remember what I said as the stamps were put into their envelopes, the albums were folded shut and the entire collection was slipped into a brown paper bag for me to take home.

I only know that I never got round to sticking them in, and that somehow, after that, things were never quite the same between Keith and me.

To claim that my school days were miserable would be overstating the case, but compared with what has happened since, they weren't a high spot. Try as I might, I didn't fit in. It seemed that discouragement lay round every corner, and no matter how hard I concentrated, logarithms and algebra remained as impenetrable as Greek and Latin (neither of which I studied, and both of which would have improved my grasp of botanical names). Enthusiasm was no substitute for the ability to master equations and remember dates. Attentive as I might try to be in the classroom, I was seldom in full possession of the facts, and after a while teachers tire of relentless enthusiasm if it is not backed up by an apparent increase in knowledge. I was, in short, a bit of a lost cause.

I wanted out as soon as possible, but that seemed an unlikely prospect. O levels were a year away, and I was staring at the sheer rock face of French and physics, maths and English, when all I wanted to do was garden. Any parent could have been forgiven for believing that these feelings were nothing more than a manifestation of idleness. After all, what teenager does want to take exams and spend every evening shut up in their bedroom with subjects and predicates, specific gravity bottles and lead shot?

Mr and Mrs Titchmarsh should have told their young Alan to knuckle down and get on with it, and in another year get an apprenticeship with a joiner – he was good with his hands and joinery was a reliable trade.

But, as luck would have it, they didn't.

Greener Grass

Y ou could have called my dad many things, but surprising was not one of them. Since the day I had told him that I fancied a life as a gardener, he had not made any more discouraging noises, but then neither had he been overly reassuring either, so the conversation came like a bolt from the blue.

'Algy . . . have you got a minute?'

He was leaning in the back doorway smoking a Hamlet cigar so that the smoke didn't go in the house. I was just coming out of my greenhouse with a watering can. It was June.

I put down the can and went through the garden gate and across the back to where he was standing. He didn't look especially cross, or especially unhappy. In fact, he seemed to be a bit pleased with himself. Mum was busy in the kitchen rolling out some pastry. I could hear her humming 'Vilja' from *The Merry Widow*.

Dad nipped out the end of the cigar with his fingers and slipped it into his jacket pocket. It always made me wince, but he never seemed to feel anything, and his jackets never caught fire so he must have done the job properly. 'We've just been down to the school.'

I feared the worst. Parents only went down to the school when there was trouble. Or a parents' evening. I knew that this was not a parents' evening.

'Why? What's wrong?'

'Nothing's wrong. Only we've decided that it might be better if you left before you took your O levels.'

I felt deflated. I know I had asked them if I could leave, but the fact that they had taken me up on it sounded as though they had no confidence in me passing any of the exams. And over the past few weeks the pressure had grown much more intense at school. Mr Smith, the geography teacher, had warned us about those pupils who left school before they had taken their exams and ended up in dead-end jobs. 'You'll hear them playing out in the street in the evening,' he said. 'Laughing and joking while you're hard at work. But put the work in now and you'll overtake them and be better off in the future. Otherwise the world will pass you by.' I didn't want the world to pass me by.

My dad continued, 'We went to see Mr Braban.'

Mr Braban was the headmaster. A thin, ascetic sort of man – a Geordie with a red face – he seemed always to carry the weight of the world on his shoulders. I wasn't aware that he had ever noticed me, or was even aware of who I was.

'We told him that you didn't really want to stay on and that you'd be happier to leave. And we told him that you were good with your hands, that you really wanted to do a practical job.'

I didn't say anything. I wasn't sure where the conversation was leading.

'We said that you were keen on gardening but that we wondered if it would be better if you became a joiner and had a proper trade.'

There he was again – going on about a proper trade.

'I see.'

'Mr Braban said that if you were unhappy, he thought it would be better for everybody – including you – if you left.'

'And became a joiner?'

Dad shook his head. On his face there was a look of resignation.

'No. He said that there are plenty of joiners in the world but that if you were keen on gardening, we should let you do that. There aren't enough good gardeners, he said, and if you're one of them, then you should be encouraged. I think that's what he said, Beff, wasn't it?'

Mum came to the kitchen door, wiping her flour-covered hands on her pinny. 'Yes.' She looked concerned. 'What do you think?'

I tried not to sound too enthusiastic. I didn't want them to confuse my glee at being allowed to become a gardener with simple relief at being allowed to leave school at fifteen and getting out of O levels.

'I'll need to get a job, then.'

'Yes,' said Mum. Then she smiled and said, 'Talk to your dad,' before going back to her pastry. Now she was singing 'I'm Off to Kay Maximes'. She always got it wrong.

Dad pushed his hands deep into his pockets. 'How are your plants?' he asked, nodding in the direction of the garden. I followed him across the back and up the steps past the little polythene greenhouse. I didn't say anything.

When he got to the top of the garden, he turned and looked back towards the house. Then he said, 'I've been talking to Wally Gell.'

Try as I might, within the brief pause before he continued, I couldn't see any possible significance in the fact that he had been talking to Wally Gell or why it might have anything at all to do with me.

'He works at the council nursery. They've got a vacancy for an apprentice gardener. I told him you might be interested.'

In one brief moment in the back garden of 34 Nelson Road on a June day in 1964, my dad went against his better judgement. He might have done it because he was persuaded to; he might still have preferred it if I had become a joiner. But I like to believe that somewhere deep down inside him was a feeling that things might just might turn out for the best. If I stuck at it.

Dad had bowed to the inevitable. You could say that it was because he wanted an easy life, or that he didn't really care what I did. Maybe I'm kidding myself, but I prefer to believe that somewhere in his heart, although he hated gardening himself, he might have felt that I was following some kind of calling. He had watched me doing it for long enough, and noticed that the keenness and the passion for all things that grew and flowered and fruited had not subsided in five years.

Although he never told me of his feelings before he died, and although we never discussed that moment again, I feel happiest when I tell myself that all along he knew what would happen. That I would prove him wrong on the one count and right on the other.

He would be proved wrong for thinking that gardening was not a proper trade. He would be proved right for believing that my love of things that grow was not just a flash in the pan and that maybe I could make a go of it as a gardener.

Whatever his reasons, I'll never stop being grateful that he gave me the chance to shine, and I'll be for ever thankful that he lived just long enough to see me making a go of it on TV. It wasn't that I wanted him to be impressed by my fame, just that I needed him to know that gardening wasn't the dead-end job he'd once assumed it to be and that in spite of my slow start I had, eventually, made something of myself.

Impressing my parents was more important to me than almost anything else. It seemed a way of repaying their confidence and the energy and effort they'd put into bringing us up during those tough years after the war. They never seemed tough to me and my sister, and it was down to my father's hard work, and the attitude of both my parents that we were allowed to grow up in a relatively carefree atmosphere, while they worried about the next meal, and whether or not the insurance man would get his money when he came to call on Friday night.

For me and my sister, our childhood was a place of comfort and reliability, and in between coping with Mum's funny little ways, and Dad's ability to side-step trouble with a brief 'Yes, dear', we knew that we were lucky to be where we were.

There are moments, all too infrequent now, when I muse on what would have happened if that contentment at being in the right place, which I felt even when I left home at the age of twenty, had persisted and I'd resisted the temptation to strike out and 'make something of myself'. A part of me – a large part of me – wanted to stay in Wharfedale. I was happy there, most of the time. There were a couple of girls I quite fancied, not that they'd noticed me, but given time, well, you never know. And when I left school early and became a gardener at the nursery, amusing myself in the evenings with a bit of singing and acting in the operatic society, it seemed that life could offer little more.

J. B. Priestley's play *Dangerous Corner* explores the circumstances that follow a particular chain of events. Towards the end of the play we are taken back in time to the moment at which one particular line sends all the characters off in a certain direction. The second time we see the scene, something else is said and their lives take a different course entirely; much less dramatic, much less eventful.

When I was still in short trousers, the world in this Yorkshire dale was as much of life as I knew or wanted to know. There was enough here to keep me occupied every waking hour, and to let me fall asleep at night with no more noise coming through my open window than that of the town-hall clock striking the hour and, when the wind was in the south-west, the sweet-and-sour smell of bracken drifting down off the moor. And yet the tang of something else in the air pulled me away from the sheltered confines of the dale. You can call it fate, you can call it ambition. I don't know what to call it. All I know is that I followed my instincts and began, in the words of J. M. Barrie, 'an awfully big adventure'. It's a childish expression, but an accurate one. And in my mum and dad's eyes, I suppose I was always a child. Their child, right up to the end of their lives.

I was walking down Leeds Road with my dad just a few months before he died, when one of his workmates shouted across to him, 'Not doin' bad, then, your Alan, is he?'

'No,' replied my dad. 'Not bad.'

Then he winked at me and smiled. 'Considering he's nobbut a lad.'

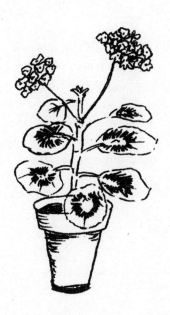